Love in Literature

Love in Literature

Studies in Symbolic Expression

Wallace Fowlie

INDIANA UNIVERSITY PRESS

BLOOMINGTON

Published in 1948 under the title,
*The Clown's Grail: A Study of Love in
its Literary Expression*, a clothbound
edition is available from Alan Swallow,
Denver, Colorado

First Midland Book Edition, 1965
All Rights Reserved
Library of Congress catalog number: 65-17792
Printed in the United States of America

CONTENTS

INTRODUCTION: the symbolism of Mallarmé's clown   7

1   FIRST CYCLE   15
   Plotinus: philosophic love   15
   Saint Bernard: divine love   22
   Héloise: human love   29

2   SECOND CYCLE   37
   Corneille: the sexuality of *Le Cid*   37
   Pascal: the attraction of the abyss   44
   Racine: the sun in *Phèdre*   51

3   THIRD CYCLE   58
   Nerval: the poet's uncrowning   58
   Lautréamont: the two monarchs   64
   Baudelaire: the sun and the abyss   73

4   MASKS OF THE MODERN HERO   80
   the 'voyou': Villon, Rimbaud, Apollinaire   80
   the artist: Proust and Joyce   96
   the pilot: Saint-Exupéry   109
   Petrouchka   113
   Narcissus   118
     i   Myth   118
     ii   Figures   121
     iii   Love   125

5   THE GRAIL'S CYCLE   128
   man: Rimbaud and Hart Crane   128
   woman: *Nightwood* of Djuna Barnes   139
   the child: Eliot and Tchelitchew   146
     i   *Four Quartets*   146
     ii   Children in the tree   149
     iii   Fire: symbolism of love   152

INDEX   155

Love in Literature

Introduction: The Symbolism of Mallarmé's Clown

GOD LISTENS TO us in the vastness of our heart as well as in the vastness of the universe. The heart is our universe of suffering. It persists in suffering from joy itself and from peace; it suffers during a global war even when it doesn't suffer directly from war. It dares to re-create each minute act of man and believe in them all with the painful and monotonous insistence of a living heart. The permanency of suffering proves that God is and that we are not in Him. It permits us to understand the immutability of God because it is reborn each day without disappearing during the nights. Human suffering is a firmament: our heart is the durable architecture which resists all the volatile and inconsistent elements which surround it. The tree of our heart exists through all the ages and grows with all experience.

Three orders of love have determined and formed the three ages of civilized man. Three orders of love, each of which has tried to retrieve the essential nature of man. Three cycles of amorous search which are drawing to a close today and which tomorrow will perhaps begin the slow unfolding of their history. Like three acts of a tragedy; like three successive attempts to penetrate the principle of life. The entire experience of man and the meaning of history are concealed within this cycle of three stages.

The need to love is the secret of living, suffering, and dying. Even in the first cycle, which is the coldest and the most serene, the philosophical cycle, man knows that love is the cause and reason of life and death, the one paradox and the one mystery to understand. He falls in love with the concept of love. Here, in the world of abstraction,

7

he wastes his soul. Plotinus is the supreme example of the human soul which blinds itself in order to give itself to that other usurping soul of philosophy. The peace of Plotinus is the great darkness of philosophic faith in God where man no longer feels any need to see in order to live.

The second cycle, which we shall call the cycle of divine love, is the one penetrated by the Christian mystics of the Middle Ages when their eyes were blinded by the total light of Revelation. Here, love is no longer a problem to dissect. It is that Reality with which the human soul unites itself. It is the testimony of Saint Augustine and Saint Bernard, the testimony of the present and of the simultaneous. The principle of divine love causes love to be forgotten because it causes no desire and no restlessness in love. Light, which is its climate, abolishes all limits and all restrictions. The peace of the saint is that light of love which is grace.

The third moment of love, which is the longest and which perhaps makes possible the other two, is the cycle of human love and passion. Experience of pain and striving; symbol of other loves; lesson of existence itself . . . In Abélard and in other men who have loved with frenzy, love dilates all the faculties. The absolutism of passion makes men explicit and bare. Tragedy ends in the total denudation of being. The magnificence of God is replaced by the poverty of the human body, but man learns thereby more profoundly than ever that he is a creature.

Love, in all its forms: philosophic, divine, human, is the residence of the Creator in His work. Man will always remain, during his life, a being provoked by God. When all is said, it is always God who acts, and man who submits.

II

Symbolism in art does not hide the artist's experience; rather, it reveals it, considering it in its relationship with the experience of races and humanity. Language is not solely the poet's creation: the symbol itself (the knowledge it contains and the purity it preserves) is another experience. The symbol of the experience is art; but the experience of the symbol is life: the life we know today and the life we knew in all centuries. Symbols are not only a tapestry of adornments, they are the living adornments of minutes and hours.

The symbol in art may be recognized as authentic if it is inexhaustible. The only experience which counts is that which can be re-created ceaselessly and which grows every day like a living force. We must appear as shadowy figures cast by the light of the symbol.

The symbol, therefore, is not only the artist's work, it is also humanity's work. (As the human body is the work of God and also the work of the soul.) It is the art of orientation and direction. The concept of time is made comprehensible by the symbol which exists for all time. In this respect, as Christ was incarnate for all time, the symbol may be considered a key to religious consciousness.

The search for knowledge in the Middle Ages was the search for the three symbolic meanings in the objects of the universe and in the created art of men. These three interpretations: allegorical, which explained the symbol according to the life of Christ and in terms of the Logos; tropological, which explained the symbol as a moral lesson; and anagogical, announcing the ultimate and spiritual meaning of every event—contained much more than the meaning of a game and even of a discipline. They represented the effort to understand and explain the experience of man. The dualism of Plato and of the Christian philosophers of the Middle Ages becomes unified in art which is the flesh and manifestation of the symbol. The very thought of Plato is the great unifying force of his dualism. The language which a writer uses is superior and incomprehensible to him because it is the language of his race and of all men. The symbol is more profound than the object symbolized.

In the Middle Ages the literal meaning of an event (as, for example, the sacrifice of Isaac by Abraham) or of a line of poetry (*nel mezzo del cammin di nostra vita*) was clear and comprehensible. The three symbolic meanings demanded more search and imagination. Saint Bernard's sermons on the *Song of Songs* immediately went beyond the literal meaning, and their creation became the life of

9

the symbol. The Middle Ages lived in the world of symbols and symbolic interpretations. The literal meaning was simply a starting point, quickly forgotten and neglected. Truth was supra-terrestrial. The literal meaning alone was clear for the artists and men of the Middle Ages, but the symbolic haunted the creative medieval mind. The symbolic was the laborious work of the mind and the imagination.

But today all this has changed. The artist continues to create a symbol, but the symbol serves also as a point of departure. The symbol is the clear and innate part of modern art. What is hidden from the artist is the literal meaning of his work, for this is the meaning he has not lived.

Let us re-read Mallarmé's sonnet, *Le Pitre Châtié*, in order to consider it as an example of modern art where the symbol is the experience and whose literal meaning probably never existed in the poet's consciousness.

> *Yeux, lacs avec ma simple ivresse de renaître*
> *Autre que l'histrion qui du geste évoquais*
> *Comme plume la suie ignoble des quinquets,*
> *J'ai troué dans le mur de toile une fenêtre.*
>
> *De ma jambe et des bras limpide nageur traître,*
> *A bonds multipliés, reniant le mauvais*
> *Hamlet! c'est comme si dans l'onde j'innovais*
> *Mille sépulcres pour y vierge disparaitre.*
>
> *Hilare or de cymbales à des poings irrité,*
> *Tout à coup le soleil frappe la nudité*
> *Qui pure s'exhala de ma fraicheur de nacre,*
>
> *Rance nuit de la peau quand sur moi vous passiez,*
> *Ne sachant pas, ingrat! que c'etait tout mon sacre,*
> *Ce fard noyé dans l'eau perfide des glaciers.*

literal translation:

> *Eyes, lakes with my simple ecstasy of being reborn*
> *A person different from the actor who evoked with gestures*
> *Feather-like the base soot of foot-lights,*
> *I cut a window in the tent wall.*
>
> *With my leg and arms a limpid traitorous swimmer,*
> *In multiple jumps, denying the bad*
> *Hamlet! it is as if in the wave I innovated*
> *A thousand sepulchres, to disappear there a virgin.*

10

Joyous gold of cymbals irritated on wrists,
Suddenly the sun strikes the nudeness
Which pure rises from my white coolness,
Rancid night of my skin when over me you passed,
Not knowing, ingrate! that my sole consecration
Was this paint drowned in the perfidious waters of ice.

For Dante (as for Saint Thomas Aquinas) the allegorical meaning of a work is always attached to the life of Christ. In Mallarmé's sonnet, Hamlet replaces Christ, or rather the *mauvais Hamlet*, the clown who is the caricature of the hero. The punished clown is the symbolic character of modern man. Painters recognized and glorified him as representative of humanity: Cézanne, Picasso, Rouault. Mallarmé's poem tells the story of an amorous temptation, but love is an experience which leads astray: it is the denial of the clown's true vocation. Solitude is the authentic ambiancy of the modern hero: he cannot leave it. If he tries to, he loses his virginity (which is the allegorical symbol of love; cf. *Portrait of the Artist as a Young Man*, Chapter 2, of James Joyce) and learns that love is an allegory, whereas Hamlet's love, the allegory of love for the modern world, is inexistent, or at least obscure and perverse. Mr T. S. Eliot, in one of his poems, says that he is not Hamlet, but rather the clown.

No! I am not Prince Hamlet, nor was meant to be;
At times, indeed, almost ridiculous—
Almost, at times, the Fool.
(*Love Song of J. Alfred Prufrock*)

This alliance of words: 'Hamlet' and the 'Fool' (which recalls the 'comme on fut piètre' of Jules Laforgue) states not only the divergence between Hamlet and the clown, but their intimate relationship. They are of the same lineage and the same race. Hamlet's personality, during 300 years, has lost much of its charm and seductiveness. Hamlet is incarnate today in Charlie Chaplin: the charm and seductiveness have been transformed into timidity and awkwardness. Chaplin's art is a new elaboration of Hamlet's experience: that of a solitary man who finds himself face to face with an incomprehensible and complex world. The same difference and the same kinship are visible in the Oedipus of Sophocles and the Oedipe of

Cocteau in *La Machine Infernale*. Sophocles' Oedipus is a virile man moved by an obscure fatality; Cocteau's Oedipe is a gigolo moved by an artist's sensitivity. The artist's sensitivity is the modern expression of fate. It is wounded daily by the world: it has ended by changing the man of the Renaissance into an insecure and pitiful creature:

> *We make our meek adjustments,*
> *Contented with such random consolations*
> *As the wind deposits*
> *In slithered and too ample pockets.*

(Hart Crane, *Chaplinesque*)

The 'random consolations' of which Hart Crane speaks, offered to the artist, prevent him from knowing a full and explicit love. The characters of Proust who give themselves to homosexual love represent a flight from the real, the fear of modern man, and his inaptitude to know life. The modern heroes all seem to live in a world of abnormality.

The tropological, or moral, meaning of Mallarmé's sonnet is translated in the clown's effort to leave himself and belie his character. Here Mallarmé's doctrine (if we have the right to deduce a 'doctrine' from an intuition which is essentially poetic) reproduces the meaning of evil according to the teachings of Saint Thomas Aquinas. Evil is our failure with ourselves, the negation of ourselves, our attempt to be something which we are not. Is not the constant effort of confessors and psycho-analysts that of discovering the true being or true personality of the patient? Mallarmé's clown, by violent action, betrays himself and condemns himself, but Hamlet fails to act. Self-analysis, for Hamlet, becomes so complete and so exhausting a world that he is unable to leave it for the world of action. Mgr Kolbe, in his remarkable book, *Shakespeare's Way*, reveals that there are one hundred and seventy passages of analysis in the tragedy of *Hamlet*. And the modern poet, who told us in a poem published in 1915 that he was not destined to be Hamlet, tells us in 1930, in his poem of conversion, of

(T. S. Eliot, *Ash Wednesday*)

Neither is the anagogical or spiritual meaning of the *Pitre Châtié* difficult to discover. It is the loss of personal salvation through evil. The first tercet in the sonnet announces a punishment from heaven. Hereby we learn how necessary it is to embrace our suffering and not to flee it. Our 'sacre' is our state of weakness which is our desire for God. But this sonnet, precisely by its anagogical meaning, testifies to a deep transformation which has taken place in the poetic consciousness: the modern anagoge is a tragedy; it was always in the Middle Ages a triumph.

In his sonnet, Mallarmé celebrated experience with the required purity. We are able to explicate in it the three symbolic interpretations, all of which exist simultaneously. But the experience itself, that is, the literal meaning, is not apparent. The literal is the most obscure meaning with Mallarmé and with the moderns in general. Progress in the world is hardly more than a progression of complications. Modern man is the clown forgetful of who he is. The literal meaning has been lost. The hero has become the weak and pity-inspiring creature who is all men.

The clown of the symbolist Mallarmé leaves his tent, swims in a lake, and thereby loses his greasepaint. Thus he renounces his 'sacre' , which is the consecration of his life. But what was this consecration? The sonnet designates the indecipherable vestiges of some strong and solid belief, as Mr Eliot's *Love Song of J. Alfred Prufrock* designates the Puritan facing the problems of love which he dares not recognize, and as *Finnegans Wake* of Joyce designates the Catholic facing the problem of a universe without faith. *Finnegans Wake*, which is the triumph of the modern creative spirit, is comparable to Mallarmé's work because its literal meaning is wilfully hidden, transformed, obscured.

III

Love, whether it be passion, or philosophy, or mysticism, is always the liquidation of a world. And a symbolic work alone contains the meaning of the trial in which man is engaged.

Art has to reveal to us ideas, formless spiritual essences. The supreme question about a work of art is out of how deep a life it springs.

(James Joyce, Ulysses)

The dualism of any profound love is resolved in the unity of great art. The history of modern symbolism is nothing more or less than the history of the secularization of medieval Christian man.

1: First Cycle

PLOTINUS: PHILOSOPHIC LOVE

W E INHERIT in our memory the memory of all men. This vast racial heritage is not always decipherable because our memory doesn't fully register the vision of landscapes and figures. We never cease wondering whether we depend solely on this knowledge buried in us, which is our memory of all past time. But we inherit also the works of men: cathedrals, paintings, poems, philosophies. In them reside the testimonials of those efforts when men tried to defeat time, when they exceeded it without being able to substitute any other subject for it. In every man slumber the forces of chaos, of love, and of universal prayer. Plotinus, in the fragments of his work which he never re-read or revised, describes these forces in terms of three kinds of men. He analyses them according to the sequence which goes from chaos to thought, which extends from unformed matter to the most impalpable spiritual adventure man can know. Thus is measured, in a certain sense, our double heritage of memory and the works of man, in which time—that force outside of man, and intuition, which is his inner force—struggle together in order to produce our profoundest moments and our most enduring works.

The philosophic system of Plotinus is the most transcendental of all systems. Thereby he is distinguished from Greek thought which preceded him, because Plotinus, a purer mystic than his master Plato, pursued solely the higher perfection. His work is not specifically Christian, but it represents such a serene moment in the conquest of the soul and such a permanent desire for union with God, that it makes possible, so to speak, the advent of Saint

15

Augustine in whom the pursuit of perfection will be the discovery of Christ's sacramental existence. In Plotinus are synthesized Platonic inspiration and the intellectual genius of Aristotle. But Plotinus lived in Alexandria which was, in the third century, the meeting place of all religions and all races. Oriental philosophy encountered Hellenic thought there, and Plotinus, master of the Alexandrian school, fused all the currents.

He was as virtuous as Socrates, his sensitivity was as nearly feminine as Plato's, he was loved for the beauty of his soul, admired because of his desire for holiness, respected for his teaching. But Plotinus was a dogmatist. Each of his sentences affirms, with an almost insolent conviction. He was one of those men who know, one of those who know love because they know themselves first. From the Greeks he inherited the need for clarity, but it was in his own nature that he discovered that need which dominated all others, and which was the purifying flame of his life: his need for unity. No other human work translates more indefatigably than the brief lessons of Plotinus which are called *Enneads*, the inner search of the soul and its progress toward realization. Before the time of Plotinus, the Hellenic ideal stretches out as on a fresco of youthful and handsome bodies, and after him, like a fresco of all kinds of human figures, unfolds the Christian drama, composed of sin and sanctity, of despair and beatitude.

The soul of Plotinus, more purely Platonic than Plato's, was triumphant over the senses. It made of philosophy a science in order to do without it and attain a goal beyond dialectics and metaphysics. His dogmatism came from his experience which was all powerful, and we seek in his writings some trace of that soul which was his, in order to contemplate a deeper reality than his words, transcribed and edited by his faithful Porphory. Plotinus was, as we all are, a prisoner of the cave, but at various moments he was able to withdraw from the spell of the eidolons on the walls and contemplate pure light. His experience was as simple as that to relate: Plotinus was the man who, among the rest of us in the cave, was able to turn his head and see the light which entered through the cracks of the door. This philosopher, who had participated in a military campaign in enemy territory, learned to detach himself from perishable things thanks to his nature which yearned for unity. 'The soul brings everything back to unity', he used to say (VI.ix.1), and this lesson, with the corollary that, alone, the being released from all vice can approach the One (VI.ix.3), inspired such saints as Athanatius, Augustine, Gregory, Thomas Aquinas.

All the names in Plotinus' language which designate God: the One, form, intelligence, the beautiful, the good, —fail, in the end, to describe Him. The God of Plotinus remains beyond the human conscience. But the desire of man and the desire of everything in the universe to return to the One (for everything that is created proceeds from the absolute) are admirably described in the *Enneads*. Desire is the theme of poets and of this philosopher of the soul. The central message of Plotinus is the patient desire of the entire universe to become God again. The reality of desire is paradoxical, in a sense, because a being which desires is not complete, but the fact that it tends toward perfection, the fact that the soul undergoes the experience of progress is so real a glory that being, thereby, already participates in the divine. In becoming a man, being passes from the infinite to the finite, but doesn't cease wishing to unite again with the infinite. The main accent in Saint Augustine's religious thought is not different from this; the bishop of Christ remained a neo-Plotinian thinker.

Desire is therefore the muse in Plotinus' philosophy, and the spaciousness we find in his metaphysics is filled with amenity and even coquetry. Every philosopher studies the mind of man through his own experience, but Plotinus studied it more resolutely and more naturally than others. His work is apart from other human creations, and his thought, as it is expressed in writing, tried to separate itself from the sensible universe.

The universal drama of man is integrally present and nobly solved in the writings of Plotinus. This drama, in every system, is invariably constructed around two questions: do we love? whom do we love? The peace and the tragedy of man depend on his capacity for love and the object of his love. All the secondary problems, to which the continuous text of Plotinus gives a soothing and unified answer, derive from these two pre-eminent questions. His lessons on the beautiful and on the mystical life are closely mingled because God is supreme beauty and above all corporeal and sensible beauty. The appearances of the beautiful, perceived by the senses, represent a fictional beauty incapable of satisfying us. The reality of the beautiful is purely spiritual, invisible as ideas, and absolute as the reality of love which is God.

Do we love? We have the right to answer yes only if we have the desire to change, to leave ourself and lose ourself in someone else. We exist by a principle of perpetual change, and we love by the desire for a purifying and radical change. Love is therefore the logical supra-human extension of the principle of life. The desire to live is instinctive and necessary; the desire to love contains all other desires and raises them to a level of divine intensity.

Whom do we love? If it is a person whom we can name, whom we have the joy of seeing daily, or of whom we think at the moments which count in our life, it is necessary then to know whether we wish, for this person, to spend abundantly our private virtues, whether we love in her not only her visible beauty, but her invisible beauty which is higher, and which, alone, is totally true. Can we know when we do this? Our conscience always knows how to distinguish between the tendency to good and the tendency to evil. When we love, we always know profoundly that the person loved is first herself and then that she is in God, being the creature of God, the reflection of His love, and the means by which we can return to Him. Love must be our desire for the person loved and at the same time our desire for perfection, which is love for that absolute beauty of which the person loved is a feeble and imperfect copy.

Thus the events of our destiny (or of our sensitivity) are measured by the love we bear. And the spiritual experience of our love will be for ever more profound and

18

more true than any human expression we are able to give it.

With Plotinus, everything is progress, evolution, ascension. Not only the most intuitive of philosophers, he is also the most phœnix-like, transforming his thought, transforming himself with the independence and the ease of a pure spirit. In the third chapter of the first *Ennead*, he describes his ascent toward the good, according to the traits of three kinds of men whose three forms of experience accomplish this vertiginous voyage of the soul. The first of these men, Plotinus calls 'the musician', and by this title he seems to mean the artist in general because he defines him as being 'moved and transported by beauty'. (I.iii.1.) The artist is sensitive to the harmony of Creation and seeks in the symmetry or beauty of his own creation a way to reach the good. He seeks the idea in its sensorial manifestations, and his happiness (or his good) is a sensuous pleasure, or what we should call today an aesthetic pleasure. 'The musician can transform himself into the lover', says Plotinus next. (I.iii.2.) The lover is the second type of man whose experience prolongs and strengthens the virtue of the artist. Of the artist in himself, the lover remembers the sense of beauty and universal harmony, but he now needs the visible beauty of a single body. He forgets for the time that the various corporeal beauties in the world are reflections of the One beauty. He is therefore that being suspended between the reminiscence of beauty and the philosophy of the beautiful. Only the philosopher, who is the third type of man in the series of Plotinus, 'has a natural disposition to rise'. (I.iii.3.) This is the third search for the beautiful and it follows the contemplation of physical beauty and the love of a human soul. The philosopher enters a still purer zone where harmony and beauty are merged with truth.

The soul, which had not been completely free in the first two degrees of this ascent, caught first by the contemplation of bodies and secondly by the love of souls, finds itself, in the third sphere, miraculously released in its new adventure of pure intuition. As before, it still feels a diversity of emotions, but they are shadowless. The soul now stops taking, and begins to create. It is beginning to feel the solicitude of the One, after having spent its time in attempting to decipher its own enigma.

The thought of Plotinus, which is dogmatic affirmation, maintains the memory of this triple adventure whose last act, however, effaces the multiple cares and ghost-like approximations of the first two. It is dogma because no doubt remains in it. It knows, because it has had the experience of all the subjects of which it speaks.

What is that zone, apogee of all adventure, where the soul undergoes the experience to which Plotinus gives the name 'ecstasy'? The phrase which ends the *Enneads* (in the order established by Porphory) is the most explicit and, at the same time, the most mysterious in the entire work: 'to flee alone toward the One alone'. (vi.ix.11.) It describes that pure act in which the soul lives freely without the shadow of any mystery, in which no gesture is useless, and where no intervention need be prepared. Even the very dreams about matter, and the unformed, and evil have disappeared! The leaving of oneself, when it really takes place, is union with God. The very figure of the soul has been born. It has found, or re-found, its function. Its cadences no longer give the impression of being invented. Identical with its principle, because it is in its principle, the soul lives for the first time with its integral life which is liberty, because it is liberation and obedience, habit and improvisation, love and beauty.

The ecstasy of Plotinus is the knowledge of tranquillity. Nothing in this Plotinian ascension resembles Christian torment or the suffering of passion. The final tranquillity attained in ecstasy is simply more profound than the initial calm and the peacefulness of inner purification. The world is surpassed, beings are surpassed, and the soul finds itself finally at the extremity of life, at the extremity of itself where it is merged in the cosmos, where it disappears in the universal consciousness. The soul which until then had slept in a human body enters a new quiet where it will not sleep, quiet which is called contemplation.

The cycle of Plotinus, this triple series formed by the artist, the lover, and the philosopher, resembles, in another order, the cycle of love, which is the subject of our study. We begin by what Plotinus discovered at the end of his search, by the ecstasy of the philosopher, which is love (or knowledge) of the beautiful without the idea of torment. Rather than representing the Plotinian cycle of artist, lover, philosopher, we intend to describe another cycle of three loves: philosophic, divine, and human— a cycle illustrated by the philosopher, the saint, and the artist. The order is thus reversed. The cycle of the patient and tranquil Plotinus testifies to an intuitive ardour which finds the form and figure of God without the love of God. The soul of Plotinus tempted God in order to prophesy its way through the obscurity of the world, after having, in the rôle of artist, tempted the universe, and, in the rôle of lover, tempted another soul.

The artist is the man for whom the word remains fresh and new. He is therefore the most 'primitive' of men, the one who lives nearest the myths and who knows the reality of each thing . . .

The lover is the man for whom human life remains fresh and new. He is therefore the most 'vital' of men, the protagonist of myths and the one who knows the death of each thing . . .

The philosopher is the man for whom ideas and intuitions remain fresh and new. He is therefore the most 'idealistic' of men, the decipherer of myths and the one who knows the plenitude of each thing . . .

The three attempts of Plotinus are joined and form a kind of cycle: art is the perpetual renewal of Creation, love is the perpetual renewal of the creating act, thought is the perpetual renewal of creating love. Each one of these heroes of the Alexandrian philosopher had his particular source of miracles: for the artist it is nature; for the lover it is a human heart; for the philosopher it is the spirit of man. The attempts are the privileges of creating, loving, and thinking. Man doesn't begin with nothing. He has no need to create something from nothingness. He begins with chaos.

To give order to chaos is the first work and the pre-figurement of that order of the mind which is the triumph of the philosopher, the flight 'of the one toward the One', in the words of Plotinus. After giving order to the chaos of matter, man tries to give order to the chaos of his heart through a knowledge of that love which will lead him to his ultimate goal. Thus Plotinus unveils little by little the native distinction of the soul. He detaches himself from everything which is matter in order to enter the liberty of the One and the promise made to his spirit by the memory he keeps of all the centuries.

SAINT BERNARD: DIVINE LOVE

The conclusion of Dante's poem accomplishes for Christian thought what the conclusion of the *Enneads* accomplished for Hellenic thought. The same experience of the union of the soul with God is announced in both works at the moment when the written words are interrupted and terminated. Neither Plotinus nor Dante tries to describe the indescribable. They both believed in a hierarchy of experiences and analysed the two ways which prepare the ultimate experience of the soul, which experience, when once begun, is silenced immediately. As Plotinus had described the adventure of the musician and the lover, so Dante described the long ways of purgation and illumination. Beatrice had led him through these two ways and prepared him for the third. At the beginning of this final way of union, Beatrice was replaced by Bernard, saint and mystic, judged worthy by Dante for the supreme rôle of advocate and initiator. This mysterious and rapid replacement which occurs in the thirty-first canto of the *Paradiso*:

> credea veder Beatrice, e vidi un sene
> vestito con le genti gloriose
>
> (*I thought I saw Beatrice, and I saw an old man
> clothed like those in glory.*)

marks the fulfilment of a psychological change in the soul of the traveller. He is now ready for the vision of God, for that experience which Plotinus called 'ecstasy', and it is Bernard, doctor of contemplation and of mystical love, who is to lead him henceforth. Saint Bernard reveals himself by name to Dante and points out to him the glorification of the Virgin Mary in the tenth heaven and the hierarchical arrangement of the blessed in the celestial rose.

Plotinus and Dante are two visionaries whose art discerns the inhabitual. (The visionary is distinguished from other men in that he lives by and for the 'accidental' in life.) The ending of the *Enneads* and the ending of the *Divine Comedy* congeal the same drama of light and create an unknown universe. We know that at the ultimate moment in both works, light, which customarily appears to men as a kind of desert, is going to be peopled. The last thought of Plotinus leads the reader toward a shining incandescence, whereas the final lines of Dante seem to sculpture light as if it were a substance.

Between these two dramas of light, between the third and the thirteenth centuries, is interposed the Christian concept of woman which henceforth must always be added, in the modern conscience, to Hellenic thought. Man is no longer separated from woman in his most spiritual adventure, as he had been in Plotinus' philosophy. Henceforth, the life of each individual man, as well as the drama of all humanity, unfolds between the actions of two women, between Eve, instrument of corruption, and Mary, instrument of redemption. At the summit of Paradise, Dante contemplates the Virgin Mary who is the last being to be known in the hierarchy of creatures before he can know divine love. Plotinus was able to approach God only after losing all contact and all memory of carnal love. The prayer which Saint Bernard addresses to the Virgin at the beginning of the last canto in the *Paradiso* serves to enunciate the pure love which Mary inspires in the heart of man. His love for the Virgin represents, in the Christian sense, the final triumph over himself and the indispensable preparation for his union with God.

The first line of Saint Bernard's prayer:

Vergine madre, figlia del tuo figlio
(Virgin mother, daughter of thy son.)

condenses the paradox of the Blessed Virgin. These few

23

syllables exhaust our intelligence and exceed it. They contain perhaps the most profound aspect of love between a man and woman. Because one woman was destined for all eternity to bear in her womb the body of God, because she consummated that act at a precise moment in the history of men, because one woman, a simple virgin, gave birth to the Redeemer, every woman must occupy a special place in the heart of God. If man is more able to worship God, woman knows God more intimately. The sin of the flesh will always appear more monstrous in a woman than in a man. The rôle of man is that of server, worshipper, philosopher, poet, but the rôle of woman is never that. Her rôle is precisely that double rôle described in Dante's line: virgin and mother. If a woman is neither virgin nor mother, she has not realized her full happiness. Carnal sin has not the same grave consequences on a man's nature.

Only one little Israelite girl was able to know simultaneously the two rôles of virgin and mother. Thanks to her and her secret action on this earth, a new place was granted to woman soon after the period of Plotinus. In the twelfth century, two parallel manifestations of this cult appear and develop: on the one hand, the profane manifestation, called 'courtly love', and on the other hand, its religious manifestation, for which Saint Bernard is largely responsible, and which is called 'cistercian love'. The glory of Dante is to have come at the end of this period and unite in his poem these two forms of love. His art is so complex and rich a tapestry that courtly love and mystical love seem to bear in it the same shadings and the same colour. Did he mingle them or have we become incapable of distinguishing them?

Between Eve, agent of alienation, and Mary, agent of reconciliation, unfolds the story of every Christian mystic. As in Plotinus, this story is a progression from light to light, an impoverishing of the world and of oneself. Courtly love, that is, love such as it was conceived in the courts, appears to us today as one stage in the evolution of love, rather than as a manifestation equal or comparable to Christian mystical love. It is true that the troubadours and the poets of the *dolce stil nuovo* seemed to accomplish a deification of woman, but in their purest poems, even in the admirable piece of Guido Guinizelli, *Al cor gentil ripara sempre Amore*, polished rhetoric exists in order to conceal a fundamental sensualism. Ovid is never completely absent from these literary expressions of courtly love, and the Lady is described as a goddess simply because she remains inaccessible and will not give herself to the lover. Cistercian or mystical love, although it is elaborated on at approximately the same time as courtly love, differs from it in a radical way. The art form of the troubadours, of Guinizelli, of Cavalcanti, is inherited by Dante. His work is its supremely mature expression, but Dante's piety and theology are close to Saint Bernard's. The songs of the *dolce stil nuovo* and of courtly love degenerated with increasing amounts of eroticism and coarseness, whereas cistercian love fermented and constructed the twelfth and thirteenth centuries. It gave them their most permanent and most glorious traits. In all domains, the Virgin Mary seems to have dominated these centuries. Cathedrals, poems, works of philosophy, treatises on mysticism—all glorified the Virgin who was Mother.

The great divergence between carnal love and divine love is explicitly defined in the divergence between courtly and cistercian love. Carnal love is dominated by fear because it is founded on a sentiment which doesn't last. The man who loves carnally can never be sure of his reward. The mystic also suffers, but his suffering is in no way comparable to that of the courtly lover. The mystic knows that God loved him before he loved God. *Ipse prior dilexit nos.* He suffers through not being able to love God as much as God loves him. In Dante's work, the difference of tonality between the *Vita Nuova* where the suffering is eminently sexual, and the end of the *Divine Comedy* where the suffering is purely religious and even mystical, indicates clearly the two kinds of suffering. *Caritas mittit foras timorem*, Saint John had written. Love expels fear, but the *Vita Nuova* is a short treatise on the familiar fear of the lover who is not sure of the object of his love.

Dante's fear at the end of the *Paradiso* is vastly different: there he shows the humility of a man who doesn't feel equal to the experience awaiting him.

This small disconcerting work, the *Vita Nuova*, is not an allegorical novel. Rather, it is the most profoundly psychological novel of the Middle Ages, and, in that sense, the most 'modern' of the Middle Ages. If the work appears to us to be pre-eminently a study of carnal love, the future development of Dante's writing is prophesied in it. For example, in the eleventh chapter, at the apparition of Beatrice, three psychological moments are described which are closely related to the three mystical ways of Saint Bernard and which are to form the three principal movements of the *Divine Comedy*. At the vision of Beatrice, Dante feels first 'una fiamma di caritade', and the flame of love has the effect on him of a purgation, which is the first mystical way. Then, all his senses, except that of sight, are overcome: 'uno spirito d'amore, distruggendo tutti li altri spiriti sensitivi'. This illumination prepares the third way of union indicated in the text by Dante's loss of consciousness: 'lo mio corpo si movea come cosa grave inanimata'.

Saint Bernard was one of those spirits who command, but despite the prodigious influence he had over men and kings in the twelfth century, he remained essentially the contemplative monk. Like Dante, he represents the two sides of the Middle Ages: the massive aspect of the Gothic cathedral and the profound spirituality of the period. We consider him the great symbol of the second manifestation of love, which we call divine love. For Bernard, as for other Catholic mystics, to consent to God is to be saved. By consent, man exercises his liberty. As a preacher, whose art has the strange vigour and sensitivity of a woman, and whose sensitivity, in certain respects, resembles that of Plotinus, Saint Bernard teaches us that there is will (*voluntas*) and also the consent of the will (*liberum arbitrium*). He tells us moreover that the wisdom of the flesh is not the madness of the spirit.

Love is always search, aspiration, impulse. It is always dominated by the supreme exigency of unity. It is the voyage with no home-coming, the loss of self which appears in every age and every mythology, as distinctly in the story of the Golden Fleece as in the quest for the Holy Grail. Love can never be dissociated from its sacerdotal significance and its mystical origin. Its experience is so impossible to describe logically and rationally that one has to *sing* it. Love is the secret which must be interpreted. It transforms men into magicians and priests and poets because it plunges its roots into the universal myth of mankind.

A single dogma intervenes between Plotinus and Saint Bernard, but it separates them fundamentally. It is the dogma of the Incarnation: *And the Word was made flesh.* If Plotinus taught that man must pass beyond the human and that the soul must be lost and absorbed in light, Saint Bernard taught that the love for our neighbour reveals to us the love of God and that God loves us in our body. The ecstasy of Plotinus is the disappearance of the individual in the One, but between Saint Bernard and his God there will always be a space and a void. It is not union with God that the Christian seeks, it is communion with Him. The ultimate and creative act of the Christian is the communion, and in this act he maintains all his being and all his personality. The full dignity of man as a being both immortal and individualized is revealed only in the dogma of the Incarnation. And it is also in this same dogma that the rôle of woman is affirmed because of the rôle of Mary in the Incarnation. In 1140, in the middle of this same twelfth century celebrated for the development of courtly love and cistercian love, the feast of the Immaculate Conception was established, but not approved of by the great doctors of the Church. It was not approved of by Saint Bernard of Clairvaux, and one hundred years later, it was not approved of, either, by Saint Thomas Aquinas. This devotion to Mary which was not defined as dogma until the nineteenth century, was first expressed in Saint Bernard's century as a deep wish of the people. It was approved of first by the humblest hearts of the faithful who wanted Mary alone among creatures, to have been born without sin.

27

If the lady of the troubadours remains inaccessible to them, and if their poetry, which at first glance appears 'Platonic,' in reality represents the sublimation of sexual desire, the other 'Lady' of the mystics remains human in her maternal comprehension of sorrow; and the devotion paid her, which might seem at first 'superstitious', confirms the central Christian dogma of the Redemption. In fact, she is indispensable to this dogma. Woman will always remain the nostalgic dream of man, because one woman gave birth to him and because the Virgin Mary gave birth to incarnate God. From a psychological viewpoint, the Freudian theory of maternal fixation in nowise contradicts the dogmas of the Church.

The sexual instinct, as expressed in courtly poetry, and divine love, as expressed in the sermons of the Bishop of Clairvaux, are two aspects of the same desire for immortality. The sexual instinct is related to that instinct for death which are two impulses toward a simultaneous disappearance, as into the night of Tristan and Isolde, whereas divine love is perhaps above all the profound knowledge that human sorrow is never useless. The most wretched and devastated lover, if he is a Christian, accepts his suffering because he knows it can *serve*, that it will help, through the mystical and mysterious exchange of graces and prayers known to God alone, the very person because of whom and for whom he suffers. If our prayer addressed to the Blessed Virgin is for a human grace, we know instinctively that this prayer, often egotistical and banal, will be converted into a very pure act of adoration, that its human element will be transformed into a divine element through the intercession of heaven's Queen.

The poet is 'courtly' because he loves what he doesn't possess, but the saint is a 'mystic' because he suffers through not loving sufficiently the One who possesses him. Poetic destiny and mystical destiny are separated by a similar excess of love which governs them: the first excess is a futile spending of passion, and the second a wealth which increases inwardly. The woman loved, whether she be Eve or Mary, is always the symbol of pure and luminous love because she is loved more when she is far away.

Saint Bernard never confused carnal love and mystical love. He knew that the first must be transformed to become the second, but he knew also that Christian theology is based upon the meaning of a universal unity. Nothing is excluded from this unity, neither fallen angels nor fallen men. Bernard was a psychologist who never remained in the realm of the abstract. In his writings, as well as in the direct action he exercised on men, he elaborated the meaning and the destiny of personality in accordance with the principle of the universality of divine love. Even if there always existed, for Saint Bernard, between fervent man and divine fervour an abyss which separates him from God, the language he used in his admirable sermons on the *Song of Songs* in order to describe the goal of man is an epithalamic language. In the saint's language the soul forms a marriage or an alliance with God in which the senses are not intensified as they are in carnal love, but in which, rather, they are liberated. 'The union of man with God consists, not in the confusion of their natures, but in the conformity of their wills.' (Sermon 71). And a supreme example of the love which man can conceive for God is the Blessed Virgin who submitted her will to Divine Will in order to bear in her womb the body of God without losing thereby her own nature or the freedom of her being.

HÉLOISE: HUMAN LOVE

No human spirit has been more supple or agile than Abélard, and more, perhaps, than Saint Bernard himself, he was the great mover of souls in the twelfth century. It is true that Bernard won out in the theological controversies, but he was aided in them by divine grace. Abélard was more dramatically alone. He was the hero of the moment, more immediately acclaimed by the crowd which loves the fervour of independence and the scintillating show of novelty, whereas Saint Bernard was the champion of the lasting cause, the representative of order and tradition, the voice which spoke to the hearts of men after the accent of his voice was silenced. The world is always led by these two kinds of spirits: by the spirit of disorder and renovation which strikes, inflames, and upsets men in some visible fashion; and by the spirit of order and meditation which influences men slowly and invisibly, and which ends by convincing and converting them. The voice of a man who is seeking God seduces men, but the voice of a man who has found God tranquillizes and changes them.

Abélard pursued the two careers of philosopher and theologian, and in each career he encountered a massive and conquering adversary. His Breton forbears bequeathed to him a passion for dialectics and an ardour for independence. His will was as flexible as his morality, but, like others of his race, like a Chateaubriand or a Renan, he knew how to incite the imaginations of men and disseminate the bitter melancholy which characterizes the Celts. He seemed always as eager to accuse himself as to defend himself, because in either position the suppleness of his intelligence could be trained and practised. His adversary in theology, Saint Bernard, whose most decisive triumph was won at the Council of Sens in 1140, came from the race of Burgundians impregnated with the constructive and orderly genius of the Romans. This same genius Bossuet deployed later in his love for universal order. But the genius of the Bretons escaped any Latin influence, and Abélard grew up with their determined need for independence and with their poetry of intellectual excitation. In philosophy, the masterful adversary of Abélard was his young pupil Héloise.

Saint Bernard reduced Abélard as a theologian, and Héloise reduced him as a philosopher. The teacher was forty years old, and the pupil was not quite twenty. He was at the height of his glory as teacher, and so renowned for his continence that Fulbert had no hesitation in confiding his niece to him and even in installing him in his own house. One of Abélard's letters to a friend, written about fifteen years after the drama and known by the title: *Story of my calamities (Historia calamitatum mearum),* is the one source of the entire episode. In this document, whose literary value has not been adequately acclaimed and which equals in certain of its pages the *Confessions* of Saint Augustine, Abélard doesn't try to excuse himself for his rôle of seducer. 'I dreamed of involving her in a love affair', he wrote first, and then, farther on, 'we passed through all the phases and all the degrees of love'. This story is too well-known to be related in detail here. Abélard and Héloise experienced the transports of a burning passion, a son was born to them, they married in order to appease the wrath of Fulbert, Héloise's uncle, who, soon after the marriage, with the help of some men, committed on Abélard the crime of castration in order to punish him in that part of his body which had sinned. The humiliation of the philosopher seems to have disappeared almost immediately. Even in the desert, where he had gone to hide his shame, he was soon surrounded with disciples anxious to hear him and exhorting him to give himself up exclusively to study and meditation. His carnal passion being extinguished even in its memory, Abélard rediscovered his original passion for philosophy. He welcomed it back as a former mistress and bedecked her with the beauties of theology. The philosopher who had become a lover now made himself into a theologian. But his real mistress didn't lose her fidelity. The physical passion of Héloise was not converted into another power. She continued to consider herself Abélard's lover and to follow out all of his orders.

Héloise didn't want marriage. She knew that marriage with Abélard, if it became known, might seriously impair his career as philosopher, and especially as theologian. She believed in a glorious destiny for Abélard, and would have preferred to the rôle of wife, any other rôle: of mistress, concubine, or even prostitute. To become the spouse of Abélard would almost equate an immoral act because she knew instinctively that sexual passion had governed her lover, whereas the passion in her was love: that is, desire, admiration, slavery. And precisely this slavery she wanted was imposed upon her by Abélard, but in a very particular way.

In obedience to Abélard, Héloise entered the religious

life and became abbess in a short time, thanks to her intelligence and example. Her letters to Abélard reveal to what degree the rigours of the cloister were for the young woman a kind of burial and expiation. It was neither devotion, nor piety that impelled Héloise to take sacred vows. It was a simple word from her former lover who wanted her to precede him in the religious life. She took the habit of a nun (as she would have committed suicide on the suggestion of Abélard) believing to prove to him thereby that he remained the sole lord of her body as well as of her heart. And she remained in the convent to expiate the brief physical suffering which Abélard had undergone because of his love for her. The act of castration which perhaps suppressed, or at least diminished, in Abélard's body any desire of the flesh, gave Héloise a reason for living. In a life of prayer advocated by Abélard, she would please him in consummating an absolute separation. 'In losing you', she wrote to him, 'I have lost everything. The infamous crime which stole you from my tenderness has also stolen me from myself.'

As a religious and as the head of a community of women, Héloise continued to play the principal rôle in a purely human drama of love. In his letters Abélard did his utmost to remind her that she was now the bride of Christ. He composed prayers for her. He exhorted her to forget their past fervour and passion in order to receive the graces which a religious life should merit. But this was vain exhortation. Héloise's heart did not change. As a last effort, Abélard wrote that he would die before her, that his body would be transported to the convent of the Paraclete where Héloise was abbess, and there, in the presence of his corpse, she would finally learn what a man is, what it really means to love the body of a man. This letter in which Abélard says that his corpse will fortify the piety of the woman who loves him, demonstrates how markedly he remained the pedagogue. After teaching Héloise philosophy and love, he wanted to teach her the forgetting of himself. And after two successes, he met with total failure. Héloise was ready to do everything except cease loving Abélard, and in one small sentence, in speaking of God, she reveals the constancy of her human love: 'I have done nothing through love of Him.' She didn't stop loving Abélard passionately when he was mutilated in his flesh, she didn't stop loving him when his dead body was brought to her convent.

The story of Abélard and Héloise has the power and magic of a myth. After the death of Pierre Abélard in 1142, Héloise continued living for twenty-one years in the convent of the Paraclete in the territory of Troyes. She kept near her the casket of her master whose epitaph was composed by Pierre le Vénérable, abbot of Cluny, who likewise wrote Abélard's absolution. As in all other myths, it is difficult for one to know exactly the final act of this love story, but it is not difficult to believe that Héloise, behind the cold walls which rose up all around her, never ceased loving Abélard. And we accept, with little opposition, the story of the death of Héloise, who had asked to be buried with Abélard. When she was carried to the tomb and the casket was opened, Abélard, who had been dead for twenty years, extended his arms toward her to receive and embrace her for eternity . . . This legend consecrates, so to speak, the triumph of Héloise and her love. During her life, she had never sought any crown of victory, and over all her nights of love, a single and eternal mirage had existed, with its illusions, its promises, its memories.

This picture of the final reunion of the lovers beyond death which popular legend doubtless created, recalls the picture of the following century which Dante celebrated in the fifth canto of his *Inferno*. The tragedy of Francesca and Paolo took place about 1285, but the world remembers it because of Dante's version placed in his poem as the introductory tragedy. The two lovers blown about by an infernal whirlwind, typifying the punishment meted out in the circle of lust, are the image of victorious passion. Like Abélard and Héloise, they remain together after death.

Amor condusse noi ad una morte
(*Love led us to a death*)

says Francesca, who is the sole speaker in the Dante episode, and this love which ends in death (because death is the sign of carnal passion) is precisely the opposite of that death which, at the end of Dante's poem, leads to Love. Francesca's line which describes the rapid possession of a heart by love could easily apply to Héloise:

Amor, che al cor gentil ratto s'apprende
(Love, which is quickly learned in the noble heart)

Héloise and Francesca, as well as Isolde, the third celebrated lover of the Middle Ages, knew and consecrated love in death. For all three, death and love are inseparable, and it is perhaps in this very equality they felt in passion and extinction that woman is the most clearly distinguished from man.

In accordance with the creation of woman, taken from the side of Adam asleep, it would seem that she was destined to depend carnally on man. The glory of woman is either the consecration of her body to her Creator, or the rehabilitation and the resurrection of the flesh. She is attached to the flesh as man is attached to the spirit. Adam was created from the dust by the spirit of God. While man keeps the memory of his creation by the spirit, woman keeps the memory of her creation by the flesh. Dante understood Francesca, as Abélard understood Héloise, but neither the poet nor the philosopher were able to feel in themselves the love which for Francesca and Héloise equals the drama of death and brings it about.

Because, then, of her mysterious birth in the flesh, woman represents too exclusively for too many men the danger of concupiscence. She seems bound to the difficult destiny of joining herself with the man she loves through a kind of exploitation of his concupiscence, while knowing—and this is the saddest part of woman's drama— that sexual pleasure is the feeblest and most insecure of all bonds. Through the voluptuousness of the flesh, which is both necessary and transitory, woman descends into the very depths of her own tragedy.

Abélard was an exceptional man and the model, as was Descartes, of those who doubt and seek. But Abélard resembles all men who are presumptuous and abundantly confident in their genius. Even as a monk, Abélard never ceased experimenting with his mind and increasing his science, whereas Héloise, even as a nun, never ceased increasing the treasure of her heart. And Abélard's genius was very close to a woman's : varied, subtle, penetrating. Man remains faithful to his search and his restless soul, but woman embraces her fidelity in suffering. 'I deserved what I suffer today', Héloise wrote to Pierre Abélard. Woman does not weep over her errors, but over those she no longer commits.

If man fears offending God, woman fears offending the man she loves, and since most women discover God in the man they love, man, in loving a woman, discovers himself in her, sees his reflection in his own traits, and plays his former rôle of Narcissus. In loving a woman, most men love only themselves. Héloise buried herself in the cloister because of Abélard and not at all because of God. And even there, in the cloister, the monk Pierre Abélard could see himself in the young prioress and abbess. Héloise remained faithful to her vocation of lover-mirror. But such fidelity shocks man (as it shocked Abélard) and he ends by denying its possibility.

Woman will usually replace man in this third part of the cycle which we call 'human love'. The humanity of woman, so maternal and so carnal, so permeated with her origin in the fidelity of union of the flesh, isolates her in this experience of love which is tragedy, failure, suffering. Héloise did not betray her first passion, which was all things for her: every form of voluptuousness, every ideal, every reason for living and dying. But Abélard traversed love, knew its gravity and power, and finally abandoned it as an experience separated from other experiences. Abélard was not solely Abélard: he was also Plotinus and Saint Bernard. Like most men, he didn't know when he betrayed himself, because knowledge of the mind and knowledge of God attracted him as intensely as knowledge of woman.

Without for one moment betraying her passion, without obeying Abélard when he demanded that she cease loving him, but in obeying all the other orders of her master, Héloise gave, even for us today, one of the purest images of human love. This image is not composed solely of fervour and fidelity and passion, it is composed also of abnegation and compassion. For man, sexual life is reduced to a series of incidents which, although often necessary and imperious, do not ordinarily form a rule of life. But for woman, sexual life is enlarged, beyond all measure, and becomes the centre and the consecration of existence. In her love for her lover, for her husband, and for her children, there is so permanent a basis of sexuality that she converts her carnal knowledge into a veritable mysticism.

With that marvellous intuition of a woman who loves exclusively and nobly but always according to the order of the flesh, Héloïse prepared to suffer. She accepted everything in advance in order not to renounce loving. To be loved thus is the deepest experience which man can have in the domain of human love. But it is his destiny to remain more detached from love than woman, to remain more free, more open to the other orders of philosophic and divine love. And this partly explains perhaps man's capacity to love the person who doesn't love him, and to give himself to the impossible. More easily than woman, man can mount the three degrees of beauty: corporeal beauty, the beauty of genius, and the beauty of the soul. The man who attains his destiny, mounts these three degrees, as the woman, who attains her destiny, remains on the first degree and, without leaving it, experiences an intuitive knowledge of the other two. The example of the Virgin, whose purity and ardour plead for all humanity, justifies the humbler vocation of other women. The blessings which don't cease coming to us thanks to the prayers of Our Lady, precede and surpass our requests. The woman whom a man knows intimately will always be for him a miracle of love because the Queen of all men and all women was a woman also.

2: *Second Cycle*

CORNEILLE: THE SEXUALITY OF *LE CID*

LIKE THE PHILOSOPHERS of the Middle Ages, the great writers of the seventeenth century in France studied man, but from a different viewpoint. The medieval study was based on man as the son of Adam, as the victim of the fall, as the creature eminently free but who is caught in the eternal debate between good and evil, and who, through his own will power, determines his salvation or his damnation. The study of the Middle Ages was theological man whose characteristics were first traced by Plato and Aristotle. But the classical study, although not forgetful of the Christian conception of man, was based on the mystery of the human spirit, on the meaning of his spiritual and corporeal destiny, on the celestial and infernal struggle for the possession of a soul. The study of the seventeenth century was tragic man, whose characteristics were first traced by Sophocles and Euripides.

The Middle Ages explain and illustrate man's anthropology, and the classical period explains the meaning of human tragedy. This tragedy which so purely concerns the spirit of man and his total destiny is enacted in a domain untouched by the explanations of psychology, of biology, and of sociology. To know oneself, for the writer of the seventeenth century, implies much more than knowing oneself psychologically, biologically, sociologically. For them, man is not a fragment of the whole, but rather it is he who contains the universe. All spheres meet in him. In his enigmatical, contradictory, and weak nature, he is able to surpass himself. This is Corneille's vision: of man in the cosmos and of the cosmos in man. His art is a new cosmic life. The common tendency of

37

man is to humanize the concept of God, but the hero of Corneille tends to divinize the concept of man. Thus, in a certain sense, these two periods of French history are distinct and even contradictory: the Middle Ages consider theological man: namely, man according to his origin and his destiny; the seventeenth century considers tragic man: namely, man in conflict with the world and in conflict with himself.

What is the domain of tragedy? We can see first that it is the domain felt and explained above all by the artists, in comparison with the domain of theological man measured above all by the theologians and the mystics. (But it must be remembered that tragic man has been understood by some theologians, such as Saint Augustine, and by some thinkers, such as Kierkegaard and Freud.) The two essential acts of God for a Christian are (1) the creation of man; and (2) the gift of His grace. Between these two divine and gratuitous acts extends the domain of tragedy, more profoundly tragic as it is more equally separated from the two acts of God. Christian philosophy lovingly safeguards not only the dogma of man created by the Divine Creator, but cherishes the belief that man, thus created, becomes, in his turn, creator of his vast and measureless liberty. We like to say today, with our impoverished and insufficient vocabulary, that the entire history of the human race is the history of democracy. This is true enough in a limited sense. But it would perhaps be more exact to say that our history is our effort to understand our freedom hidden in the mystery of those abysses which existed before historical time.

Corneille is the initiator of a movement of ideas and of a chapter in art which begin roughly with the birth of the seventeenth century and which are perhaps destined to terminate in the cataclysms and the global revolutions of our own age. But since he was initiator, Corneille didn't progress very far in the domain of tragedy. He makes us feel it, however, in all his plays, and especially in *Le Cid* which we are going to use as example, by his persistent use of the triumph of grace. Corneille violates tragedy by insisting on the large amount of spirituality which inhabits each one of his great heroes. Rodrigue and Chimène are two children who announce all the forms of modern tragedy without succeeding in incarnating them explicitly. Markedly absent in them is any expression of terror, the sentiment which Kierkegaard defines in the nineteenth century as the eminent sign of spirituality in man. Even the women in *Le Cid* do not feel terror. Chimène isn't terrorized by the murder of her father and the appearance of Rodrigue in her own house. She feigns terror, as an actress would, but the primitive vigour of her joy and her love wins out over all the inferior sentiments. The Infanta, more purely tragic than Chimène, doesn't discover terror in herself, but rather that form of despair which henceforth will be the vice of modern spirituality.

No terror, then, in the virginal world of Corneille because purity abounds there. It is almost as if the Creation had just taken place, and that at the end of the twenty-four hours with all their fatiguing peripetiæ, joy would be reborn, greater still because it would be the joy of grace after having been the joy of creation. In the middle of the Cornelian play there occurs the tragic moment which is rapid and immediately over. It is the moment of the fall, the return to the void which existed before the creation. The moment of vengence felt by Rodrigue and Chimène, even if it is at once annihilated and surpassed by them, is sufficient to make out of this poem of love, a tragedy. Vengence is called by anthropologists the oldest of moral emotions, and can be traced back to the most primitive periods of history. Vengence exists because man is not only a being created by God, he is also a personality. Our personality is our oneness, that part of ourselves opposed to what is mortal in us. Christianity teaches us that personality exists because of the sentiment of love. The sentiment of vengence breaks out in man, only to hurl him toward the void of the fall, because of the collective personality of the clan which is innate in primitive man. This sentiment, which is very concealed but real in Hamlet, is born instinctively in Rodrigue and threatens his happiness in accordance with the formal law of tragedy. For a moment in the life of Rodrigue and Chimène, they

39

forget themselves in order to sacrifice to the cult of the family and the clan, because of some primitive blood mysticism, their personal happiness and their love. This ancient instinct of collective responsibility toward the social group or the race has been converted by Christianity into the dogma of personal responsibility for the sins of all men and into the universal love of Christ in his mystical body.

Therefore, the principle of paternity, oldest of all principles, against which Oedipus had fought, is the first principle in *Le Cid*. The primitive character of this tragedy is clearly drawn in the effortlessness with which Rodrigue abandons and surpasses the principle of paternity which had engaged him during the first two acts. In the third act, he becomes a man in love, tormented by the drama of passion and sexuality, incapable of finding peace because the principle of sex divides man against himself and fills him with horror. In the fourth act, Rodrigue becomes a creator and enters upon his destiny. He channels all his sexual force and surpasses it in one great act of heroism. The triumph of the battle with the Moors is the triumph of sexual sublimation in Rodrigue, as a great creative work in someone else, in a Leonardo for example, is the same kind of triumph. The principle of man is always an effort to deceive his sexuality, to do without woman, to remain faithful to his 'solar' principle, which is his principle of creation and fecundation. But Chimène doesn't renounce as willingly as Rodrigue the principle of paternity. She is clearly the woman who safeguards the communal idea and the perpetuity of the race. What is for Rodrigue a question of honour, is, for Chimène, the instinct of a woman, the instinct of maternity and procreation. The sun, a phallic symbol in its evolution and its force, is opposed to the earth, symbol of woman: of her maternal flesh and of her cosmic meaning. Whereas Rodrigue traverses the work of Corneille with the sword of his spirit and the solar force of his youth, Chimène remains stable during the entire play as the antithetic principle of man, as the symbol of matter and the collective unity of the earth.

Man doesn't succeed in destroying the sexual urge of his nature. If he doesn't give himself over to a free expression of his *libido*, he can hide it and suppress it in the obscure and sometimes dangerous recesses of his subconscious, or he can surpass it, sublimate it in a great spiritual act of creation or heroism. Thus, the hero, like the creative artist, transforms his sexual *libido* into an expression of power which the theologians call *libido excellendi*. Rodrigue in the second act, in his victory over the Count, and in the fourth act, in his victory over the Moors, struggles not only against his love for Chimène but against the very principle of woman. He affirms himself in the play as a single personality who opposes the maternal element, the earth, the community, and the primordial instinct of sexuality in his being. Rodrigue goes against everything once he discovers the fathomless liberty of human nature, once he discovers in his own subconscious that the principle of man is that of the logos and the creation and is eternally opposed to the principle of woman which is that of the earth, of procreation, and reproduction. Rodrigue, like all heroes and all great artists, has to struggle against the sexuality of his nature, not because of some point of honour, which critics explain so often and so insufficiently in the tragedies of Corneille, but because of a much more profound reason. He knows, at least in his subconscious, that sexual satisfaction is the source of life and death, and that there is in man a more imperious desire than that of life and death: it is the desire to triumph over life and death (desire which women do not know), to preserve and keep intact all of his sexual vigour.

If Rodrigue struggles for the freedom of his male spirit, in order to free himself by surpassing woman, and if he fights the Moors not through patriotism but in order to escape the monotony of domestic quarrels and forget himself in an adventure of danger and chance, Chimène renounces every struggle once she has chosen her rôle of matriarch representative of the clan, in order to throw into relief Rodrigue's struggle. She stabilizes the earth and the cosmos, and then she patiently waits for the prodigal to return to her arms, as to the source of life and to the maternal centre from which he tried to escape in the rantings of his youth as well as in the very passion of his love. Rodrigue is the eternal man pointing out the possible ways of the future and all the circular movements of the sun and of the spirit, who affirms his personality in the very presence of Chimène. She is the eternal woman revealing the vast and solid shelter of matter and community, the tranquil site of our genesis, the earth and the womb, the final repose of man devoured by restlessness.

'Je ne t'accuse point, je pleure nos malheurs', Chimène says to Rodrigue in their great scene of the third act, and her conscience is almost at ease. But in her subconscious she favours a sadism, which is another feminine principle. (If Descartes, at the time of Corneille and *Le Cid*, taught the psychology of consciousness and reason, Freud has shown since then the far greater importance of the conflict between the conscious and the subconscious faculties in man). Chimène torments others and rejoices in tormenting them, not through some point of honour, but because of a very ancient origin of primitive suffering. Rodrigue, more masochistic than Chimène, as most men are, knows that happiness is not the conscious goal of men. In loving Chimène, Rodrigue loves sorrow; he loves a good and not a happiness. Woman holds unto the past and prays for the present to stop. She opposes time and change because she is eternity, whereas man represents the triumph of time over eternity through his autonomous acts of heroism and violence which, once they are committed, die and disappear in that past he wants to create and from which he hopes to liberate himself.

Each human being has an androgynous nature and develops through the union of the masculine and feminine principles, through the simultaneous existence of personal passion and communal sentiment. In that nature where equilibrium between man and woman is quite sustained, the effort to realize oneself and surpass oneself is sharper, more uninterrupted, more necessary. Tragic sentiment is easily created in it because this nature, conscious both of its personality and of the cosmos, favours so equal a struggle between the two principles that no

42

triumph is assured. This kind of human nature lives under the threat of itself, anxious over the responsibilities it feels toward the entire world and toward its own heart. *Le Cid* offers to us in Rodrigue and Chimène two beings fashioned very lucidly in accordance to the two principles of man and woman, but in the character of the Infanta, Corneille depicts a more purely tragic nature in which the two worlds of man and woman face one another and devastate one another. Chimène and Rodrigue speak only of blood, of swords, and of immolation: blood to avenge and blood to shed are the two constant themes of their speeches which make of *Le Cid* a kind of mediaeval tournament. But the voice of the Infanta heard as early as the second scene of the first act and not silenced until the second scene of the fifth act, that is, the voice heard just after the beginning of the play and silenced just before the end, is the voice of modern times and of our heroines today. Her voice gives the work its true tragic colour because she is alone in the labyrinthic complexity of her heart. She is indifferent to vengences and thrones, to the sportive and youthful struggle between Chimène and Rodrigue. They don't cease for a moment loving one another: they remain therefore very near to the creation of their love and they await impatiently the moment of grace destined to consecrate their love. They traverse so rapidly the domain of tragedy and with so much exuberance so weakly controlled, that they hardly perceive the domain itself. For them, the story is a bad day in their lives which will be quickly forgotten. But the Infanta, each time she appears on the stage, performs the eternal gesture of tragedy: she opens on herself the gates of death. Because she is not loved, she possesses all the cruel leisure necessary to understand the double principle of love: its expression of life and death, of life which, for her, is death, and of death, which is life. The Infanta, in the eternity of her waiting, of her despair, of her courage, and of her goodness, is a counterpart of the Blessed Virgin who is the eternity of grace, the awareness and the fecundity of grace. There are traits of Héloise in the Infanta in the image of her long fidelity, and traits of Hamlet in the restlessness of his nature, and

43

traits also of Phèdre in the potency of an impossible love.

In a sense then, the Infanta came into being in spite of chronology, because Corneilian tragedy is the triumph of grace. Even *Le Cid*, because, of course, *Polyeucte* is a more obvious example. *Le Cid* is the story of Chimène who symbolizes the plenitude of the cosmos and the female element of the earth; and then, *Le Cid* is the story of Rodrigue who returns to Chimène after leaving her. He symbolizes the return of the sun to the maternal principle of the cosmos, to the principle which sustains and renews the earth. Thus, the Corneilian solution resembles a philosophic love which rediscovers the equilibrium between man and woman, and which, after arousing sentiments of theatric fright, arouses in their place sentiments of veneration and calms the impermanent virtues. The earth absorbs the heat of the sun in much the same way that Chimène envelops the intrepid passions of Rodrigue. The plenitude of the cosmos ends by covering the principle which pierces it and fecundates it.

PASCAL: THE ATTRACTION OF THE ABYSS

If it is true that Descartes and Pascal represent the two poles of French thought, the two inexhaustible sources of reason and restlessness which have fashioned the two forms of French genius, the one in its clear logic, and the other in its insensate dream which is independent of logic; if it is true that all movements of the French soul before the seventeenth century are renewed in the philosophy of Descartes and in the thoughts of Pascal, and that all movements since then, all the disinterested aspirations of modern man as well as all of his personal and cosmic problems reflect the precise form which Descartes and Pascal gave them—the world today, after listening attentively for two centuries to the lesson of Descartes, seems ready to consider with more benevolence and more fervour the intact lesson of Pascal (although it is the most fragmentary of all lessons).

Pascal feared any triumph of reason as if it represented a failure of true human greatness, as if it manifested an evil which was constantly intent upon perverting the heart. Alone among the thinkers of all periods, alone among the great thinkers and saints of Christendom, Pascal feared human reason and refused to seek assurance. All his life he remained the frail child, restless and sick, whose heart triumphed over every intellectual vanity. His spiritual disquietude was neither the cause nor the effect of his physical malady, but it made of Pascal, who, incapable of sleeping, watched over the world with Christ, the most tragic poet of France. Pascal's moment, which has been called the 'classical' moment in the history of the French soul, followed the Renaissance, characterized by the intoxication of knowing everything, and preceded the century of the philosophers, characterized by the certainty of knowing everything. Reason in Rabelais and Montaigne was confused with imagination, because the great minds of the sixteenth century tried to forget and transform and even trick the hard and fatiguing dialectics of the Middle Ages. Later, reason in a Voltaire, forgetful of its order and its rigour, served ideas like some sharp instrument, not in order to demonstrate but to kill. Pascal lived briefly between these two periods when reason, rather than serving and sustaining man's faith, as it had done during the Middle Ages, behaved first like a spoiled child, like young Gargantua who at birth cried out 'à boire, à boire', and then like a steel blade whose sole use was to massacre.

But to say of Pascal that he was the enemy of reason would not suffice. He was also the enemy of all carnal concupiscence and all ambition. In fact, reason and concupiscence are so exclusively the themes of Pascal that, since his time, thinkers and artists can no longer consider man triumphant over the weakness of reason or the specious traps of concupiscence. In the history of ideas, Pascal's work interrupted the current of Platonism. At each period since the dialogues of Plato, some manifestation or other of mystical spirituality has recalled them: Plotinus and Porphory in the third century, Saint Augustine in the fifth, Boethius in the sixth, Saint Bernard and the Provençal poets in the twelfth, Marguerite de Navarre in the sixteenth. But since the time of the dizains and the religious poetry of Marguerite, what author has been purely Platonic, with the very doubtful exception of Santayana in the twentieth century? Pascal has become so intensely the poet of the abyss, symbol of the void which surrounds every man, and from which the Platonic soul had turned away in order to contemplate God, that the peace of the spirit—the very reason for the fear-inspiring poetry of Pascal—is his unwritten book. Pascal never removed his iron belt. The darkness of his abyss was so complete that it touched and altered the Christian experience, and, in fact, the philosophic thought of our own time. Pascal, who would like to have composed a new illumination for the work of Plato, cast over the various beliefs of men the darkness of his personal anguish. This anguish of the abyss which was first that of a solitary man, became the universal anguish of an entire culture. In the great modern works of the human spirit, Pascal has replaced Plato. Plato had his disciples in Saint Augustine, Saint Bernard, and Dante. Pascal has his disciples in Baudelaire, Kierkegaard, Joyce, Eliot, Mauriac.

Pascal still watches over the world in the artists and thinkers who seek because they have found. The Pascalian lesson on the abyss was not so much for the world a lesson as a creation. It continues to exist substantially among us, and we are born, if not in the centre of the Pascalian drama, at least under its shadow, with the memory of a mute universe and with the haunting recollection of a *Deus absconditus. Les Pensées* are a creative work and not a discourse or the synthesis of a discourse. If Pascal was one of those men desirous of propagating their word, he was also one of those who work according to the inflexible principles of art: sublimation of personal life in the work, decantation of personal experience, discovery of oneself in the analysis of one's own spirit, equilibrium between the meaning of created form and the memory of all the past.

Before Pascal, creative power was manifested above all according to the principle of antithesis: body and soul in Plato, hell and paradise in Dante, Thélème and the monastery in Rabelais. But after Pascal, the principle of metamorphosis is substituted to that of antithesis: Phèdre is not opposed to innocency, she is a woman possessed and transformed by desire; the 'déguisements fantasques' of Verlaine have their origin in Baudelaire's theory of 'make-up' (*maquillage*); H. C. Earwicker is doubled and replaced so often in *Finnegans Wake* that we end by hearing him without being able to see him; the innumerable faces of children in Tchelitchew's tree play at a *cache-cache* so profoundly metaphysical that the work overflows with all the themes of the modern spirit and mingles them in the new correspondence of 1942, which are the transformed memories of all preceding correspondences.

Baudelaire had clearly understood the Pascalian drama when he wrote in his sonnet:

> *Pascal avait son gouffre, avec lui se mouvant.*

One can feel in the great Christian spirits before Pascal, that evil for them was something exterior, a force waiting for them, but outside of them, foreign to their life, even if it constituted their permanent danger. But Pascal's abyss lay in his very being. He engendered it every day by means of some principle of a mysterious and terrifying marriage. His implacable drama was the renascence and the responsibility of the collective drama of man which tormented his nature and filled it with hallucinations and metamorphoses. All faces looked at him because he had them all in himself, and no one face was dear to him inwardly, but the abyss they filled was a mirror reflecting grimaces, dreams, insolences. No love in the obscure light cast by all the centuries of doubt and reason. No love, that is true, but one must add immediately, no dissolution either. Therein lay the greatness of Pascal.

All is vanity, all is uncertainty, even the love of Jesus Christ, the one truth that is known, which, like everything else in this world, despite the efforts of Pascal the geometrician, is not demonstrable. Like the faces of all the children in Tchelitchew's *Cache-Cache*, the innumerable proofs of Pascal built up by reason to abolish reason, still exist today and do not cease transforming us because

47

they participate in that gratuitous game we call art. Pascal still lives, not because of his apology for Christianity and his revolt against reason, but because of his soul tormented by the infinite and the absolute. Pascal's soul was the noblest apology of Christianity, because no one ever dreamed of demonstrating it. His abyss was as purely symbolic as Tchelitchew's tree. The abyss and the tree are in equal measure the origin of the cosmos for the thinker and the painter—the same obscure point out of which everything will come: sufferings and children's faces —as well as the unfolding of the cosmos which contains all the experienced sufferings and all the children who both look for one another and avoid one another.

'La Sagesse nous envoie à l'enfance', Pascal wrote, in alluding to the passage in Saint Matthew: *nisi efficiamini sicut parvuli* (*Matt. xviii*.3). But to become again as a child doesn't equal a defeat of reason. That first imagination where we exist in a kind of delirium or ecstasy is the triumph of reason, and later in one's life, when 'nous sommes pleins de ténèbres', as Pascal wrote, we try to recapture it. The only 'proof' found by Pascal was his abyss. Men know the hell of Pascal, even if they can't accept the bargain he proposes: 'Si vous gagnez, vous gagnez tout; si vous perdez, vous ne perdez rien.' Pascal the logician attracts and moves us much less than Pascal the martyr. And the child, which Pascal was all his life, which Rimbaud was in his most visionary hallucinations, which Stephen Dedalus is in his search for a father and in his meditations on the complexities of Hamlet (cf. Joyce, *Ulysses*, p.182-215), which the clownish children of Picasso and the childish forms in Tchelitchew's painting are— the child is the great martyr whom his imagination and his inner life crush according to some propitiatory principle. Long before Rimbaud, whom the surrealists of the twentieth century have proclaimed leader, prophet, and seer— Pascal, the most naive of thinkers (who are often startlingly childlike), composed, during a malady comparable to a permanent state of madness, one of the most terrifying books of surrealism, or at least based on principles which artists today jealously designate as 'surrealist'.

48

Rimbaud's 'dérèglement de tous les sens' is called in Pascalian language 'l'abêtissement de soi'. The heretics, logicians, and pyrrhonists, so implacably opposed throughout *Les Pensées*, are called in *Une Saison en Enfer* teachers, priests, merchants, but the two authors, the one as cruel and fanatic as the other, are speaking of the same enemy, he who pretends to be interested in the truth, but who in reality denies the boundless and sorrowful imagination of childhood.

The revolutionary force in France seems to be heard at each period in two voices and two spirits: just previous to the scholastic period, it was Abélard and Saint Bernard; before the classical period, it was Montaigne and Pascal; before the surrealist movement, it was Hugo and Rimbaud; just before the global war of the twentieth century, it was Gide and Claudel. If we are not sure, in this enumeration, of the fairness of each name mentioned, we are more sure of the artistic and intellectual tendency which these names represent. In each case, two men, or rather two kinds of mind or two kinds of metaphysics, are opposed in their philosophies whose principal mission is to conciliate and synthesize the very age they predict and prepare. The first author of each annunciatory group— Abélard, Montaigne, Hugo, Gide—designates the negative revolutionary spirit. Very different from one another in art and sensitivity, they are related, or at least reminiscent of one another, in their critical accomplishments. Abélard submitted the representative men of his period to a rigorous examination. He operated on them, so to speak. Montaigne, Hugo, and Gide perform the same exploratory work and pose again, each in a manner suitable to his age, all the principal problems of man. What unites these four leaders is their criticism of the very construction of the thought, the axioms, and the major hypotheses which were directing the men of their moment in history. Each of these thinkers announced to his generation the ideas which were no longer tenable. But the other group, represented by Saint Bernard, Pascal, Rimbaud, and Claudel, announced not a revolution of ideas, but a revolution of sentiment and of the heart. Rather than wishing to effect a division in the minds of men, these authors of the second group advocate a deeper awareness of all ideas, a clairvoyant study of our heritages which will put everything in its place according to a more authentic and more stable hierarchy. Evil will therefore have its place beside the good, because in this world good is incomprehensible without evil. Reason divides us inwardly: the *Essais* (Montaigne) of the sixteenth century, as well as the *Journal* (Gide) of the twentieth century illustrate this principle. Alone, the secret of the heart can lead us to love. The *Pensées* (Pascal) of the seventeenth century and the *Odes* (Claudel) of the twentieth century support this law of man made in the image of God.

The Cross of Christ is sunken into the abyss of Pascal and keeps it eternally opened. No man embraced the Cross more passionately than Pascal. His love of God is his love for the Cross. The two Pascals, the poet and the scientist, are united in a single love. And this Cross which Pascal embraced without ever sleeping during the night of the world, is the one symbol for the two truths of Christian faith: God and the corruption of man. Alone, the Cross was intelligible for this man who felt, before fighting them, the pride of philosophers and the despair of atheists.

Love is that universal energy which transforms the physical passions of man into a creative force: Pascal constructed from his abyss, which the Cross of Jesus filled so exactly, the pure geometry of his *Pensées*. The agony of Jesus never permitted the agony of Pascal to reach a measureless depth. The Saviour's agony precedes, surrounds, and surpasses the agony of any man who seeks salvation. Thus, divine geometry triumphed over the Pascalian geometry of love because it contains the key of every problem.

The agony of Jesus on his cross dictated to Pascal, bearer of his abyss, his most poignant thought: 'Nous ne vivons jamais, mais nous espérons de vivre.' The love of Saint Bernard, ineffable for having exceeded the agony of the world, gives way, four centuries later, to the love of Pascal, tortured through not feeling itself fully Christian. The love of the contemplative saint, a supreme example

50

for all the Middle Ages, gives way to the sick child whose testimonial has not ceased affecting the modern world. The tears of joy shed by Pascal on the twenty-third of November, 1654, were the tears of a child who, alone among men, could know Jesus because Jesus was God and his agony.

RACINE: THE SUN IN PHEDRE

Each age is comprehensible and distinct according to its doctrine on human suffering. In the seventeenth century the evolution of this doctrine forms a unified and complete lesson. The hero of Corneille seeks his happiness and safeguards it in life and in death. Pascal, a tragic hero like Horace and Polyeucte, sought for his salvation and safeguarded it in the suffering of his body and in his spirit tormented by the agony of his God. The heroine of Racine completes this evolution because she seeks not only to destroy herself but to destroy all those who exist around her. If Corneille seeks to avoid suffering and Pascal to embrace it, Racine represents the triumph over suffering and the immeasurable widening of its domain. He represents the human heart finding its pleasure in suffering, jealous of every unknown agony and form of sadism.

After the image of man always accompanied by woman which Corneille gives us, and after the solitary humanity of Pascal, Racine offers us the image of solitary woman. Hermione, Bérénice, Phèdre are alone with themselves, but they keep the memory of the species and preserve the meaning of continuity. Each one of his heroines appears on the stage bearing over her features the mask of eternal woman, eternally alone, eternally necessary to man who turns his back on her and escapes from her. At each entrance of Phèdre, the stage becomes empty and she remains alone with her memory peopled by its own species, alone before all the elements of nature, alone as if she were some bewildered victim who had wandered away from her executioner.

51

The first words which Racine has Phèdre say, her first apostrophe which never ceases resounding throughout the tragedy, her

soleil, je te viens voir pour la dernière fois,

announces everything. The radiation of the sun is the permanent symbol of tragedy in Phèdre. The triumph of the sun—it is at the zenith when Phèdre comes to contemplate it for the last time—first marks the tragedy. The sun is not only the ascendency of Phèdre, since her mother, Pasiphaé, was daughter of the Sun—it is also the triumph of man in his phallic symbolism, the piercing power of the male which Phèdre in her woman's flesh cannot extinguish or embrace. The sun, at first a god for Phèdre to whom she is bound by close consanguinity, is above all for her the image of young Hippolyte who mounts with the day like a corporeal star and descends into the night to fill it with his presence and his memory.

At the beginning of the play, Phèdre appears under the full light of the sun, and it is impossible for her during all the unfolding of the tragedy to retire within the shade, to sit down, as she longs to, 'à l'ombre des forêts'. Rather than diminishing, the force of the sun grows in each act. The soul of Phèdre grows more and more shining under the solar rigour, and at the end of the work, the intensity of suffering, which is intensity of light, reaches the moment of conflagration. Phèdre perishes in her own flames. The tragedy ends in a chemical and supernatural fire.

Phèdre herself never becomes, even for an instant, the sun. She never leaves the purity of her own drama. She is always the victim of love, of the sun, and of man. She is the victim who receives, if not the fecundating and real force of love, at least its imagined and cruel force. She receives, during this one day of the tragedy, all the superabundant energy of the sun, as if the energy of the cosmos was being spent for her in some effort of nature to perfect divine creation by destroying her. Racine created in his work a solemn and terrible cult. The sun-ravisher strips Phèdre of her clothes and leaves her nude before the eyes of the spectators. Each line she recites, as in some propitiatory sacrifice, translates an act of the sun perpetrated on her flesh and on her soul. Before our eyes she is slowly consumed by the love which strikes her in the heat and the light of the sun. The force which Phèdre would like to have felt in Hippolyte, she feels in all of nature which rushes through her in flames of poison. Love is not for her a man, it is the sun incapable of appearing in a human and desirable form. The supernatural surrounds Phèdre and wards off the natural.

When she learns, in the fourth act, of the love of Hippolyte for Aricie, and when jealousy, the new and final suffering, is added to her passion, Phèdre, in her most poignant line, evokes the innocency of that other love by means of a familiar image:

Tous les jours se levaient clairs et sereins pour eux.

The passion of Hippolyte and Aricie unites them in a love comparable to the light and the justification of the day. The world of men welcomes this kind of love, as the universe welcomes the return of the sun, but Phèdre, who seeks to flee the light, cannot escape from the sun before falling inert and consumed by its force. Alone before the sun, Phèdre presents to it the flesh of her body and suffers even in the memory of all her race. The sun captures all the agitations in the being of this woman who, during the moment of her race when it was permitted her to live, dared oppose the celestial fires and arrest their burning menaces. This was Phèdre's struggle against the natural cosmos and against the divine order of the cosmos. Her disorder, which is felt, imperceptibly at least, by all beings, is suppressed by them and relegated to the secret parts of the subconscious. Most men prefer to forget or destroy such a passion rather than to live in the vast solitude it exacts, with nature itself, the sun and all the stars, as the eternally vigilant enemy destined to triumph.

Phèdre is never separated from her heart, as most men and women are daily. Her tender and terrible faith is reminiscent of the solemn perfection of Jansenism, that philosophy of man in which Racine as a boy had learned to touch the most intimate secrets of the heart. Phèdre is not a criminal because her love for Hippolyte is not literally incestuous, but she foresees the crime for the future

53

and at the same time she dreams of the past. She dreams of her mother and thereby suffers for all the maternal sins. This is the way in which horror and monstrosity stifle Phèdre. She deceives us, and we believe, in listening to her, that passion is incorruptible. We learn to believe that this daughter of Pasiphaé has warded off all the angels of the resurrection and that she will always remain faithful to her flesh, accomplishing her mission of fidelity to the earth, eternally remembering the rocks and the trees, dissimulating nothing of what is in her nature and no part of the sun's dark action on her.

But this drama of the flesh ends in the drama of purity. After the first scene when Phèdre remains alone with the sun composed of her ancestors, of her heart, and of the terrible future, and after the central scene when jealousy heightens her passion and transforms her soul into a site of paroxysm, comes the final scene when Phèdre, in the presence of the spectators, and her ancestors, and all of nature, enters death while experiencing for the first time in her body an unknown coldness, and while converting her heart into a purity worthy of rivalling the purity of daylight. The last speech of Phèdre resembles the poison which is flowing through her veins and diminishing all the signs of life in her body. Her very words denude and transform the meaning of life. Only material substance counts, and the words are lost in the new conversion where flames triumph over the body and where Phèdre fails for the first time to see the sun because she is entering it in the midst of her ancestors. This final drama of purity is the congenital catastrophe where Phèdre, after struggling against the cosmos, is assimilated by the cosmos into its most immaterialized sphere.

The principal action of Phèdre is therefore not so much her attack against modesty as her struggle against the sun which she is forced to look at and which is destined to destroy her. Racine understood above all in the character of Phèdre the maternal and primitive trait of woman who struggles for the preservation of the race and whose tragedy is the loss of self before the re-creation and justification of self. Every woman is tragic who is unable to

54

become, in her racial and solemn rôle, mother of all men and history. The absolutism of passion, manifested in Racine's Phèdre and in Shakespeare's Cleopatra is the absolutism of the void and of ashes, that absolutism which crowns both works in the implacable resolution of the final purity. Purity absolves the passion of Phèdre and Cleopatra by destroying it, even in its memory.

Woman is with the race and creation, but man is alone, more tragically alone. That is why the tragedy of a woman, alone with her passion and incapable of converting it or appeasing it in accordance with the simple and practical law of reproduction, appears more monstrous than all the tragedies of men. Phèdre and Cleopatra both have in their speech a sequence of words which describe the evolution of their passion: its unfolding and its death in the cosmic fire:

Phèdre: acte   I: soleil—forêts—horreur—crime—fureur— Vénus—proie.

      acte II: fureur—abhorrer—feux—monstre.

      acte IV: douleur—rebut—crime—inceste—soleil— enfers—bourreau.

      acte V: incestueux—funeste—poison—jour—pureté.

Cleopatra: act I, scene 5: mangragora—treason—eunuch— poison—unpeople.

      act II, scene 5: eunuch—barren ears—melt gold— serpents.

      act III, scene II: blown rose—cold heart—poison— stone—pelleted storm—graveless.

      act IV, scene 13: sun—knife—drugs—serpents— heaviness—melt—withered garland.

      act V, scene 2: ruin—ditch—naked—abhorring— cinders—ashes—marble—fire and air.

The two tragedies of passion contain a similar evolution in their imagery. In *Antony and Cleopatra*, it is progress from fertility to dissolution, and in *Phèdre*, it is progress from desire to dissolution. For Cleopatra, love is at first symbolized by the earth and the mud of the Nile, and at the end of the tragedy, it is vaporized into flames and into the air. The transformation which Phèdre undergoes is similar, because the transports of love she feels at the beginning of the tragedy are metamorphosed into the purity of day. The love of Phèdre and Cleopatra was always death, but it is called by its real name for the first time at the end of the tragedies in the purgation of all the terrestrial elements. Born from passion, Phèdre and Cleopatra expire in passion.

Both tragedies describe a cycle of overpowering and total passion. Phèdre, goddess and lover, personifies the terrible unity in love and death exacted by the gods and the psychology of woman. Cleopatra, actress and lover, personifies the diversity in this unity. For Phèdre, the sun is lover and executioner, beginning and end of an experience which wilfully destroys her in agreement with the orders of the gods and of men. For Cleopatra, the Nile and the fertile lands periodically covered by the waters of the Nile symbolize the love of abundance she claims, but this same soil, when it is used and worn out symbolizes the exhaustion of love. The language of Phèdre mounts toward the sun until the moment it catches fire and is extinguished in the flames. The language of Cleopatra descends toward the Nile and the over-rich lands of the Nile until the moment it loses its form in the viscous slime.

Phèdre is a profoundly religious work. An eschatalogical work. As the heroine's language mounts toward the sun, the meaning of sacrifice becomes increasingly clear. At the conclusion of the work, Phèdre appears as a victim suspended between heaven and earth. The victim and the target of the sun.

> *Thy face*
> *From charred and riven stakes, O*
> *Dionysus, Thy*
> *Unmangled target smile.*

(Hart Crane, *Lachrymae Christi*)

The stake of Dionysus, god of vegetation, of wine, recalls the Cross of Jesus, God of men. But in the last scene of Racine's tragedy, the body itself of Phèdre is a stake and a cross while it becomes for an instant the target of men and of the gods. Dionysus, in expiating passion, is the target of the world's concupiscence; Christ, in expiating sadism, is the target of the world's sin; and Phèdre, who will be replaced in the nineteenth and twentieth centuries by the artist, in expiating pride, is the target of the world's cruelty.

The fury of Phèdre is impossible to conceive without the dogma of grace. Grace exists by its absence in the tragedy of *Phèdre*. It is grace which, absent or present, places on the face of a woman her tragic mask. Without grace, Phèdre would be purely a woman and would not be that creature we know solicited by all the demons and all the angels. Without the concept of grace, Phèdre would resemble Molly Bloom who, in the long soliloquy at the end of *Ulysses*, sings solely of the carnal and cosmic principle of women, and reproduces the circular movement of the earth, the natural history of the cosmos, the woman waiting in her bed for her husband and who is going to say yes to him in adherence to the instinctive law of the species.

In the heroes cf Corneille, carnal passion is subordinated to the passion of order: it becomes in Rodrigue, and to a certain degree in Chimène also, philosophic passion. In the thought of Pascal, love reproduces the order of charity in which man surpasses himself, after he had been made greater, purely as man, in the universe of Corneille. In Racine, love seems always to equate self-annihilating passion. Phèdre incarnates tragic passion which is dissolved. Thus Corneille, finding what is noblest in man, announces Pascal who, finding outside of man what is divine, yields his place to Racine who finds in man what is most corrupt.

As if what is corrupt in man hasn't the right to exist, Racine prepares for the final scene a conflagration in which the whole being of Phèdre, contaminated by evil, burns and loses its form. And this woman, who had never renounced the spirit during her dream of the flesh, rediscovers in death that purity of spirit which the saints rediscover in life through their denial of the flesh.

3: *Third Cycle*

OR MOST OF the romantics, the dream world was a second domain of consciousness to which they escaped with pleasure, where they fought reason and reasoning, and where they bedecked, according to their desires, the real world. The dream for Chateaubriand, Lamartine, and de Musset was a band they put over their eyes to blot out the vulgar world of the bourgeois. For only one of the romantics was the dream what it should have been: the world of the subconscious controlled by its own laws, where the inhabitants are indigenous and bear the recognizable traits of fantastic and fairy-like creatures. The name of this romantic, Gérard de Nerval, is as unreal as the visions which compose his dreams, and after one hundred years, we say today 'Gérard de Nerval' and read the sonnets of his *Chimères* and his short novels, as if his true name and real life outside his writings had never existed. The dream of Nerval has triumphed. His work, rather than being an obviously symbolic transcription of his life, is his life. Everything has been reversed in Nerval, because his life is a faint transcription of his dream.

As the popular ballad reveals the heart of a people more accurately than any historical narration of events, as mythology alone really penetrates the meaning of history, Nerval's work, and especially the sonnets called *Les Chimères*, form a more authentic record of his life than any biography could. The sonnets are much more than a distillation of experiences. They create the new compact life where the settings are more real than the landscapes of the Valois and the Orient, where the characters are more living than Adrienne in the children's dance in the park of the château, and more real than Jenny Colon on the stage of the Paris theatres. The voyages in *Les Chimères* are the only ones we need to follow. The madness of this poet undertook voyages less exaggerated than the real voyages in which Nerval, incited by his studies of the cabala, of magic, and mystical initiations, destroyed the real worlds. His wisdom was obscure because it was composed of magnetism, esoterism, and occultism, but his madness was lucid because it constructed the limitless and perfect world of dreams. As a traveller, Nerval pursued the symbolism of numbers and the memories of magic and of cabala, but as a poet, he constructed the existence of a man who loves and suffers. Any historical or psychological method used to explain Nerval will fail, because reality for him existed as the substance of a dream, as a substance to be modified and remodelled. His writings are therefore as invulnerable as a dream. Any explication is less than approximate. In order to read Nerval, it is a question of living a dream and feeling its beauty. It is not a question of dissecting it.

The figures of the women who inhabit his work resemble those phantoms who are always the same phantom of a dream. Adrienne, Jenny Colon, the Neapolitan girl, the English girl, are all synthesized in Aurélia, the only woman Gérard could love since, never having seen her in life, he was able to make her divine. The conscious life of the poet was composed of departures, of voyages, of peregrinations, and only in his dreams did he remain immobilized before the ideal form of the woman he was seeking. A poet of love, Nerval always remained a poet of metempsychosis: he was never sure of loving, he was never sure of having loved, and only in his dreams was his former existence of Eden purity, of innocency, and of happiness reproduced. Nerval encouraged his madness because it abolished time and plunged him into a distant past where all was illuminated with joy. The children's dance during which he received a kiss from yellow haired Adrienne marked the beginning of an experience in metempsychosis in which he believed he was all the youthful dancers of former times and in which so ancient

59

a ceremonial kiss symbolized perfect happiness. The moment of ecstasy in our childhood, which was perhaps in Gérard de Nerval's case, Adrienne's kiss, is the supreme moment in our amorous experience which we try during the rest of our life to recognize, to recapture, to re-live in other forms and with other beings. The spiritual experience alone of love is tenacious. It inevitably triumphs over physical experience in binding us to time which has gone by, to a past which becomes present and future. Love is metempsychosis. It is the same experience we re-live ceaselessly.

> *La treizième revient . . . C'est encor la première.*

The sumptuous resonances of this sonnet of *Artémis*, while knowingly falsifying the truth, reduce the fragments of real experiences into a single experience as simple as it is profound, as permanent as it is inaccessible.

Artémis is a luminous example of lyric creation in which the entire life of the poet is recast: all the idealisms and all the failures. The sonnet not only contains direct reminiscences of nocturnal life, of death, of youth, and of maturity—it reproduces at the same time, and through that miracle of coincidence and evocation which art alone can construct, the universal experience of all men. *Artémis* diminishes life, in re-creating it, by use of the simplest words in all languages: 1. treize et premier; 2. reine et roi; 3. berceau et bière; 4. aimer et mourir; 5. rose et sainte. Paradoxically speaking, Nerval succeeds in doing in his sonnet what James Joyce does in *Finnegans Wake*, in the numerous closely covered pages of a long work: the re-creation of a life and of life. In each group of these primitive words of the sonnet there exist worlds of involuntary memory. The subject matter of *Finnegans Wake* is these worlds, silenced in Nerval's sonnet but obscurely living in the imagination of each reader. A work of art, truly, is not constructed on a subject matter; it is infallibly constructed on an absence. The void left by a completed experience is the authentic subject matter of art, and in a literary work, words come to fill this void without however building a real substance. An experience becomes spiritual especially from the moment it is translated into a language. Art consecrates

60

the spirituality of life by giving it a form, as the body consecrates the spirituality of the soul.

The principle of metempsychosis (revealed in the first line of *Artémis*, in the meaning of the words 'treizième' and 'première') abolishes, by surpassing it, the tragic notion of love.

Et c'est toujours la seule—ou c'est le seul moment.

'The one moment' referred to was that love always sought by Nerval because it had once existed and because it continued to exist in his dreams. This dream is as imperishable as life itself, bequeathed to all men according to the mysterious principle of the survival of souls and things. Tragedy is therefore only the arresting of life and the death of dreams. Nerval never entered tragedy because his dream was an uninterrupted communication with the past, the survival of experience, the reality he asked of every day and every night. Nerval's poetry first abolished tragedy because of the fact that experience is never terminated, and then abolished time, effaced by the very character itself of dreams.

I am ready to believe that Nerval was one of those very exceptional men whose thoughts are always pure. The purity of his imagination is almost unique in literature. It prevented him from becoming tragic. The tragic hero is the victim who has encountered his executioner. But Nerval was the victim without an executioner, eternally extended on the altar, living, behind his closed eyes, the drama of life and death. Both his dream and his sorrow were virginally modest. Lying on his altar where all possible voyages haunted him, he could see in his mind's eye the subtle skies of the Valois, the foggy forests of Ermenonville, the campestral landscapes of Mortefontaine and Loisy. Incapable of living or dying, Gérard tried to identify himself with all the characters in life and in death, and to feel the destiny of each one in order to fill the abyss extending around him in all directions.

Si je meurs, c'est que tout va mourir

he said in one of his sonnets on *Le Christ aux Oliviers*, and therein stated one of his most purely nihilistic philosophical thoughts. In this line, he expresses his identity with the cosmos. In him cohabit the natural and the supernatural, and after him all will cease existing. The dreamer is a victim, and the worlds of his dream gravitate around the void. Nerval's work was an appeal, not for the purpose of justifying before his friends and physicians the attacks of madness which constantly threatened him, but for justifying his thought on the abyss and on renascent love. As the perpetual vagrancy of his life led to suicide, his limitless dreams coincided with the death of the worlds, with the extinction of the dark suns of melancholy. Metempsychosis ceased to be for Nerval a religious principle and became a principle of delirium and poetry. I believe that Nerval didn't like living. He had no real desire to live, as most men have. His mind, ornamented solely with his dreams, lived by not living. As Jews are specialists in catastrophes, as Americans are specialists in optimisms, Gérard de Nerval was a specialist in dreams. He knew neither sun-fed passions, nor obscure loves. He only dreamed passionately, obscurely, wilfully exhausting the vision of a children's dance which appears both so darkened and illuminated that it is accepted as an incomprehensible rite of some lost truth. Nerval played the rôle of lover as a guardian or a priest who had never seen his goddess or his god. Nothing existed for him in time: neither heaven nor earth; neither love nor faith.

The tragic hero of antiquity, of the 'chansons de geste', and of the classical theatre, is abstemious of words, but Nerval, in pursuing the reality of language, pursued at the same time the reality of dreams and avoided the tragic or glorious conclusions with which life is composed. Thereby Nerval is the ancestor of *Le Grand Meaulnes*, of Proust, of Bloom. No modern poetry is more 'narrative' than *Les Chimères*. The principle of illuminism penetrates the entire work of Nerval and is opposed to any ultimate light, either tragic or sanctified. Nothing ends, neither life nor death, because men and gods equally never cease being absorbed in the universe. The final substance of the sonnets—all the very simple words and the pauses between the words and the lines—is the only immobile element in

Nerval's work. This substance chained to the·white pages sings of perpetual becoming and recommencing where tragedy is an episode, where glory is a disappearance, where death is life.

Romanticism, of all the centuries and not solely of the nineteenth, is the dream of life, the harsh and provocative disproportion which exists between imagined life and daily life. Rousseau, in certain pages of his *Rêveries*, bequeathed to the hyper-sensitive hearts of the nineteenth and twentieth centuries, ways and exercises by which to attain the ecstasy of dreams, but the Rousseauistic romantics in their dream of life are today replaced by Gérard de Nerval in his life of dreams. The climate desired by Jean-Jacques was the dream of nature, but the climate desired by Nerval was the nature of dreams. The human solitude of Rousseau gave way to the mortal solitude of Nerval who felt, more profoundly than the Swiss writer, the desert truth of the cosmos.

The love expressed by Nerval at the inception of the modern era is love of eternity, love of that force which bends trees and men, but which also straightens them up thanks to the indestructible truth of dreams. The poet Nerval knew himself as a living man and as a future dead man: he did not distinguish in himself the two rôles which are measured by the two rites of life and death. Uncrowned by life, this prince of Aquitania was crowned by death. It was fitting that at the birth of the theatrical romantic pessimism in the century which has given the greatest number of dreamers to the world, a single writer should cease contemplating from his real site the clouds of his dreams in order to live in his dreams the transfigured image of his life. Like Plotinus who, immobile, contemplated the drama of his being, Nerval contemplated love, without loving, without living in love. Like the heroes of Corneille who, forging the destiny of their duty, dream of the love which will one day be accessible to them, Nerval dreamed of what a calm and reasonable life might resemble, while forging the limitless kingdom of his dreams.

One of the major characteristics of twentieth century literature is its preoccupation with the child and the theme of adolescence. Artists, in accord with psychologists, have believed that childhood and the period of puberty have peculiarly penetrating insights into the world of the human spirit as well as intuitions about the destiny of man and the complexities of his being. Announcements of this new literary mine were numerous in the nineteenth century: Nerval, Hugo, Stendhal, Sand, and countless others dealt intermittently with the child or the youth. But two names above all others are associated with this theme: Lautréamont and Rimbaud, because they achieved, before their youth was over, a literary testimonial of their experience. The poetry of Rimbaud written between his sixteenth and nineteenth years, and the prose of Lautréamont composed when he was twenty, are without precedent in literature. They are not the fumbling ill-constructed statements of inexperienced but gifted young writers, nor are they logically formed inquiries of mature writers. They fit into no category. Distinctly autonomous, although there are literary sources for both works, they flare up brilliantly and briefly, almost in the same years, in the midst of a period dedicated to bourgeoisism and realism. They are works of revolt and passion, but so centrally the universal revolt and passion of mankind, at once so primitive and civilized, so deeply rooted in the eternal problem of good and evil, that they are difficult of comprehension in any usual way. They were almost born as myths and not as ordinary literary creations. And like myths they preserve secrets deep within them. A myth grows out of facts imaginatively and prophetically interpreted. In the fashioning of a myth an entire people, joined together as though they were a single artist, re-create a simple historical fact with the boundless imagination of a child. The case of Rimbaud, both his apparition and disappearance, has been laboriously explored and analysed. He is an established poet now of importance even if critical writings and exegeses on him contradict one another, even if we fail to understand much of his sensibility and the real problem of his metaphysics and of his nature. But the case of Lautréamont still remains unexplored.

Those who have loved him the most, the surrealists, have made of him a kind of mysterious deity and patron. Breton, Aragon, Eluard — and, before them, Apollinaire and Max Jacob, have so venerated Lautréamont that any profane explanation of his significance would seem blasphemous. Wilfully they have kept him a 'secret' which can be apprehended only by the initiate. In a sense, he is the symbol of incommunicability, a projection of that mystery which has fixed itself on many forms of modern art to such an extent that the art resembles a new ritual testifying to a reality which, like any religion, must be 'experienced' rather than apprehended intellectually, and believed in rather than explicated according to the laws of reason or logic. The poetry of Mallarmé and Rimbaud, the paintings of Picasso and Braque, *Finnegans Wake* of Joyce, *Four Quartets* of T. S. Eliot, are all examples of modern art which require, on the part of the spectator, for any participation in their beauty and meaning, a long preparatory period of veneration and implicit belief.

Even the very life of Isidore Ducasse, who preferred to call himself 'Comte de Lautréamont', is an enigma. And even those surrealists who have believed in him without talking very much about him, have been unable to discover anything about his impenetrable life. Beyond the simple facts of his birth in Montevideo (Uruguay) in 1846, his coming to France about the age of fourteen, his studies in Tarbes and Paris, the publication of his first *chant* in 1868, and his death at the age of twenty-four in 1870, literally almost nothing is known about him. The hypothesis of Lautréamont's insanity seems to have been instigated by Léon Bloy in his sentence: 'L'auteur est mort dans un cabanon, et c'est tout ce qu'on sait de lui.' (*Le Cabanon de Prométhée, La Plume*, 2e année, pages 151-154.) Whether or not Lautréamont was suffering from dementia precox and the beginnings of schizophrenia can never be established. The artist or the genius inevitably appears mad when compared with the ordinary man; it might even be said that the bourgeois appears just as mad to the artist as the latter does to the bourgeois. Lautréamont's excessive love for mathematics (cf. *Deuxième chant de Maldoror:* 'O mathématiques sévères, je ne vous ai pas oubliées.') and his love for the piano may have helped to channel and transform his strong emotions. His face, as it emerges in our imagination (for there is no portrait whatever of the real Lautréamont) is that of a tragic mask, but it is that form of tragedy which marks the seeker of the absolute. Whereas the poetic imagination of Lautréamont is reminiscent of Dante, the Marquis de Sade, and Blake, the mask covering his features so closely that it has become them, is that of a Pascal and a Saint John of the Cross.

Les Chants de Maldoror relate the monstrous struggle of a man with his God. The fear of damnation is all the more strong as a theme because it is never expressed. The setting is the entire world reduced to a wilderness because nothing real remains outside of the mind and the tortured conscience of Maldoror, the last in line of the romantic heroes. He accomplishes their destiny for all of them, releases them from their minor pettinesses, and raises their lesser struggles against nature, woman, society, to a theological level. Maldoror doesn't oppose man as his romantic forbears did, he opposes God Himself and assumes the rôle of modern Prometheus or Lucifer. The consciously designed mask he wears is that of a sadistic frenzy. He tests himself, like any novice hero, on experiments in cruelty and sensation, but each act of sadism is offset by an act of compassion. No human experience exists for him between a knowledge of cruelty and an extreme form of tenderness. Maldoror rides through the night on his horse, like some strange mythic monster, in revolt against the unknown, yet on his way toward the unknown. The romantic hero has finally become the epic hero, fighting for the cause of man against the Creator of man. But already in this monstrous revolt of man against God, God is triumphant. Maldoror emerges from a moment in history when the doubters of God were legion, when by his affirmation of God's hate, he unconsciously subscribes to God's love, because in himself love and hate exist in equal force and equal passion. In *Les Chants*, God and Maldoror are two neighbouring monarchs, one fearing the other, God Creator of Maldoror, Maldoror creator of his hate for God, and thereby testifying to the reality and the existence of God.

The madness of Maldoror was as necessary for the renascence of God in the modern consciousness as the madness of Rousseau was instrumental in God's exile from the nineteenth century consciousness. The madman who remembers God from an earlier lucidity is more dangerous than the madman who comes upon God in his insanity even if he misinterprets the character of God as he misinterprets the character of every other being. In the last analysis, the world is led spiritually by the abnormal, by the slightly deranged who is genius, artist, prophet. It is obvious today that modern art, which is the gauge of our thinking and sensibility, has been influenced and formed by the partially insane: Nerval, Hölderlin, Baudelaire, Lautréamont, Dostoievsky—rather than by the more obviously sane: Voltaire, Hugo, Renan, Zola. If the great are not directed by an inner madness, an outer exile, like that of Dante and Joyce, may develop their lucidity. There is perhaps a strong relationship between the paranoia of maniacs and the imagination of a Lautréamont. Both kinds of fever may be the necessary admission to a realm closed to the sane and the healthy, to a Voltaire-the-professor who at best can only take notes on an experience he has never had. Love is no worldly fiction for Lautréamont; it is a celestial reality which he acknowledges by his very denunciation of it.

Maldoror, as the genius of evil, equates his sadistic impulses with hate since they give to his nature its most heightened form of expression. And therefore pity, which is the reverse of sadism, will be for him the major expression of love, or the good. But since Maldoror is obsessed, these values, to understand their real perspective, have to be reversed. When this exercise is performed and the terms recast, pity appears in its real meaning of sadism and hate, and sadism in its truer connotation of love and self-donation. Any form of insanity, as well as a sonnet of Mallarmé or a painting of Picasso, is a profound synthesis and new expression of values. But beneath the synthesis, and jealously protected by it, lie all the familiar motives and all the often-rehearsed laws of love.

Maldoror manifests, then, the strength of a hero in his sadism, because hate is the perversion of love and always capable of righting itself. But in his moments of compassion he diminishes his stature, because pity is a camouflage for vice, the subtle manifestation of *acedia*. A hero can feel no pity; he must slay. A saint may feel no pity; he must love . . . At one point in the second *chant*, when Maldoror contemplates in the sleeping hermaphrodite the beauty of virile and virginal adolescence, the sentiment he describes is not pity but love. And he fails to recognize that this new sentiment is simply the reversal of his customary hate. He is obsessed, as Hamlet was, with the desire to comprehend his feelings, and is puzzled when, in his experiences of pity, he is unable to distinguish between good and evil. Pity acts as a drug upon the will and arrests its functioning. Maldoror's revolt is absolute; love and hate are welded together into a force with which he can love man and hate God.

In a sense our childhood is a statement of our mature subconsciousness, as an artistic work is a statement of man's absolute. And as a man cannot be explained by his conscious thoughts and deeds, so a literary work cannot be explained by a knowledge, no matter how profound, of the man who created it. All song is a transfiguration, and Lautréamont's, if it seems to be composed with the criminal coolness of a Lucifer, bears also in itself traces of angelic innocency and love. Angels and youths stalk through its stanzas, impervious to the abundant blasphemies. This invulnerable purity of Lautréamont's angels and boys is proof that his blasphemies are ornaments and that his hate is love.

The rôle of poetry is perhaps, when all is said, the simple harmonization of the child's sensitivity, dormant in man's subconsciousness, with all of his experience. If Lautréamont considered most of his century's poetry 'sophismes' and 'gémissements', it was because he felt it lacked the primitive understanding and vision of a child. Surrealism has been, to a large extent, the revindication of the child's world of intuition and symmetry, the involuntary analysis of the microcosm and of all the epochs of culture and consciousness which coexist in every individual being. From the sonnets of Nerval to *Finnegans Wake* this is the history of western literature, and midway in this period, *Les Chants de Maldoror* occupy a strong pivotal position. Poetry has become the study of the secret of being. Rather than calling it ontology, it would be more appropriate to call poetry the secret of ontology.

This secret of ontology which Lautréamont felt and his nearness to the reality of God are the distinguishing characteristics of his work. He appears to us today as the most aristocratic of all the French 'voyous', vainly hiding behind his second personality of noctambulist and vampire. In fact, his second personality was all personalities: he was 'comte' as Nerval was 'prince d'Aquitaine'. But he succeeded more completely than Nerval did, in losing his identification. His portrait, both moral and choreographic, becomes so complex that it is unrecognizable and his pose of noble voyou is covered with the flames of some infernal haughtiness and grandeur. The features of Nerval remain clearer because he kept before him some image or other of the woman he loved, but Maldoror, having no one to love, found only hate in his nature and projected this hate into the various characterizations of himself.

God reads the books of the poet and considers the work of the genius. But behind these works of men, which have had to be created in accordance with the laws of fabrication and technique, God can also contemplate the creative fire of love which is their origin and which has been cooled down when the lover becomes creator. The deep sadness and dissatisfaction of the creative genius when his work is finished is ample proof of the infidelity to his experience he has been forced to traverse before becoming the literal

69

creator. His sadness is his memory of love and of its imperfect reproduction in art.

Lautréamont's art, as well as the art of the surrealists and particularly of such painters as Chirico, Chagall, and Matta, testifies more directly to the pure origin of the experience which was spiritual and not technical. Surrealism is a closer approximation to the secret of the spirit than other forms of art. The freedom of evil, which is at the origin of our human life, explains why our primitive spirit and subconsciousness can be so peopled with monsters. The astounding scene in the second *chant* of Lautréamont where Maldoror copulates with a female shark after a bloody slaying of other sharks, seems to rise up from that abyss of the spirit into which we seldom look after our childhood. The horrible fusion of the swimmer's body with the shark's, which Maldoror calls his first love, is symbolic of that frenzy and of that memory of evil which lie at the beginning of each life. These visions of our original nature we tend to palliate whereas the surrealist resurrects them with a child's ingenuousness and almost with the child's ignorance of their meaning. Lautréamont is one of those geniuses who did not forget how monstrous our dreams are in reality and how we rationalize and conventionalize them in conscious reminiscence.

In the tenth book of his *Confessions*, Saint Augustine describes an amazing proof for the existence of God. God must exist, he says, because he has come upon Him in the vast palaces of his memory: *et venio in campos et lata praetoriamemoriae* (x.viii.12). And later in the same passage he defines memory as being the spirit itself: *cum animus sit etiam ipsa memoria* (x.xiv.21). This is perhaps the first portrait of man the microcosm who can resurrect in his memory all epochs and who can even return in his memory to the period before the creation. In his memory of the creation itself Saint Augustine discovers among the characteristics of God His paternity and loving kindness which became in the synthesis of Saint Augustine's theology a principal tenet for Christianity. Later-day surrealists might well return to the *Confessions* for doctrinal confirmation of much of their psychology and theory concerning creative freedom. God for Lautréamont also, is the Creator, and he acknowledges Him because of his memory of their burning kinship. But Lautréamont's memory of God the Father, so luminously clear in the memory of Saint Augustine, has become blurred in the European consciousness. God is still the Creator, but His laws design the grotesque. He is the buffoon who has fashioned human beings in a tragic moment of mirth and perversity. Here Lautréamont's memory is playing tricks on him, and he is confusing the First with the Second Person of the Trinity. Christ is the eternal clown, the passive scapegoat and caricature of our desires and our dreams. It is kinship with Christ the buffoon and not Christ the Creator that Lautréamont feels in this important passage of his third *chant* which is a tragically modern counterpart of the tenth book of the *Confessions*.

The genius is always closer to the First Person because he is the image of God the Creator. But the saint is always the transfigured creature and clown, the counterfeit of Christ the crucified. Whereas the saint directs his life toward personal salvation and therefore keeps his eyes fixed upon Christ who is the means for his salvation and the Divine Clown eternally exhibited before mankind, the creative genius, unconcerned with salvation or damnation, mimes in his creativeness the acts of God the Creator. The genius renounces himself because during his acts of creativeness he is somehow plunged into the period which preceded the Fall. Lautréamont's image of God and man as two neighbouring monarchs is really the image of two rival creators, of two creating spirits both free in the acts of their creation, both suspended in that time before the Fall of man when there was no need for God to incarnate Himself in the crucified Clown and no need for Maldoror to contemplate the Cross as the unique symbol of defeat and triumph.

With the innocency of a child, Lautréamont stepped out of the period we designate as history. And Arthur Rimbaud did likewise. History is man's freedom in good and evil. The end of history will be the end of this freedom. And the period before history we can only call the

71

period of God's creativeness. But into some fictional replica of that time-before-history Lautréamont and Rimbaud entered. Their freedom from good and evil was almost consummated there, because they ceased being men choosing freely between good and evil, to become personalizations now of good, now of evil. Their hardness, the glazed brittleness of their language, their mask of cruelty which grew over their youthful features to protect the tenderness which the world has never learned how to understand, all testify to a self-discipline which is the perversion of asceticism. Rather than engaging in self-flagellation, Lautréamont and Rimbaud undertook to flagellate themselves in their Creator.

Love had to be whipped because Lautréamont and Rimbaud, before knowing it, had deep premonitions of its suffering. As we read their story in the frozen stanzas of their self-flagellation in God, we see more and more clearly the contours of the strange myth from which their experience springs. From the myth before time and from before the incarnate expression of love. Every man, even if it is only for an hour or a day of his life, experiences the reality of that myth. The myth of the void is as true as the myth of the creation, and for the creative artist, the first myth, that of formlessness and nothingness, is the most terrifying story of mankind. 'J'ai reçu la vie comme une blessure', writes Lautréamont (third *chant*), and we sense that the hollowness of a wound, in his image, equates the terror of the void and of formlessness. He failed to recognize that the creation of form on the part of God was an act of love and that the petrification of the world he describes in *Les Chants de Maldoror* is apprehended only by a heart which has ceased loving.

Love is form. A creative work of man is a victory over life in much the same way that form is the victory of order over disorder. If the form of the universe appeared to Lautréamont unreal and distorted, it was because love, the indispensable basis for form, had not been achieved in him. In his century, order lay about in ruins, and these ruins were visited by Maldoror. The necessary will toward form, intimated by Lautréamont, was more clearly apprehended by Rimbaud. But the work of both, reflecting the force of evil, or what we prefer to call the ruin of form, marks in the nineteenth century a reversal in literature from a useless denunciation of evil to a knowledge that evil can be opposed only by the one force stronger than itself, which is love.

BAUDELAIRE: THE SUN AND THE ABYSS

The drama of Eden is at the centre of every art, and, in the poetry of Baudelaire, it is re-enacted as if bedecked with a total modernism and stripped of all accessories, like some religious celebration of primitive times. Baudelaire was an authentic Adam, protecting deep within himself the memory of his innocency, and seeking everywhere except there where it resided in the ancient garden, the purity of his desires.

The voyage undertaken by Baudelaire is much more than the romantic revolt and the modern evasion of the neurasthenics. It is the prayer of a man in exile, immobilized wherever the good does not transform objects and beings. Dante's voyage was likewise a prayer, intact and architectonic, preserving the three proportions of failures and promises and salvations. Don Quixote's voyage for the deliverance of the world; the voyage which Hamlet, a seductive and melancholy contemporary of the Spanish voyager, hesitated to undertake; the interstellar voyage taken so often by Nerval; the voyage of twenty-four hours in Dublin taken by the Jewish Ulysses; and so many others, ridiculous or heroic, real or imagined, all repeat the same search and the same need, all celebrate consciously or unconsciously the same goal.

Man is gigantic according to the concept wherein life is envisaged as a series of real or desired departures: we must believe in all the voyages man doesn't undertake. The truth of the familiar life he wishes to leave is a second mother, comparable to the woman who gave him birth and from whom he must separate himself. The falsehood of the voyage thus becomes the comedy of life because it hides, in the adolescent and in the man, a feeling of inferiority which a man will spend his life in disguising. The voyage is therefore the comedy which takes place between the time of promise, which is birth, and the time of accomplishment, which is love or death. It matters little whether in the voyage man crosses a physical part of the earth or whether he remains immobilized in the centre of himself. The latent lie which precedes all our acts illumines the truth of the voyage's goal. The lie explains the truth, as the comedy explains every final and tragic act.

Baudelaire's *Le Voyage* is composed of many stages. The child he evokes in his first line, the boy who is 'amoureux de cartes et d'estampes', seems destined to know:

1. the true voyage 'sur le fini des mers';
2. the voyage of the conscience in 'le spectacle ennuyeux de l'immortel péché';
3. the voyage of the senses in 'le Lotus parfumé';
4. the voyage of purity when 'nos cœurs que tu connais sont remplis de rayons';
5. and finally, the voyage of the unknown and the new which terminates the poem and which represents the poet's greatest desire.
6. To these five stages of the Baudelairian voyage of comedy, we should add perhaps a sixth which is the Baudelairian voyage of tragedy, described in *Les Plaintes d'un Icare* where the poet, having before his eyes only 'des souvenirs de soleil', becomes a new Icarus. This is the definitive voyage, for, 'brulé par l'amour du bien', nothing remains to Icarus, neither his life nor his being.

Between the first voyage of the child where his pure and transforming imagination surpasses the reality of a map or an engraving, and the last voyage of Icarus where the hero is consumed by the sun as in an orgasm produced by the copulation of the void with the void, are enacted the slow and ugly gestures of the comic voyage. The inalterable subject matter of *Les Fleurs du Mal* is the vision of the albatross, not free in the heavens, but ridiculous and captive on the deck of the ship. It is the vision of the swan, not free in its lake, but escaped from its cage and bathing its wings in the dust of a Paris carnival. The voyage which tortured Baudelaire and which he had to undertake through some imperious fate, was the martyrdom of exhibitionism. The albatross, the swan, and the poet are the same exhibitionist suffering before the eyes of the entire world in accordance with the principle of his nature. And during his martyrdom, this exhibitionistic Adam doesn't stop addressing reproaches to God.

A voyage is generally undertaken because of two goals which are more or less concealed in the mind of the voyager. The first of these goals, which is often announced, is a mission, either the mission to save others or the mission to save oneself. The second goal, which is usually unarticulated because it is often not fully clear to the voyager himself, is the erotic desire to exhibit oneself in an unfamiliar place, before strangers. Baudelaire's voyage, which he speaks of in *Correspondances* as well as in *L'Invitation au Voyage* and in *Un Voyage à Cythère*, never accomplishes a mission. The poet never really takes his departure, but he shows himself to each of his inner landscapes and reveals himself before each character who lives there. Baudelaire's spiritual voyage was a voluntary and cruel exhibitionism enacted before himself, more ferocious than all the banal romantic chastisements, more bitter than the literal departures of a René or of a Manfred. The need to exhibit oneself is the narcissistic deformation of the need to love and be loved. Baudelaire shows his suffering, his sensitivity, and his spirit to the void because the places he visits are not real and the character he sees there, the mistress and the madonna, do not exist. The places he visits on his voyages are the fountain of Narcissus, and the faces of the prostitute and the muse which he sees there are the features of the poet himself, the reflections of his spleen and his ideal. Bending down over his own reflection, the poet travels everywhere and never leaves himself. What other space could he traverse except the immaterial cosmos of his heart where the milestones collapse as soon as they are touched, like the deceiving substance of a dream ?

*　　　*　　　*

The drama of Eden, immobile and tenacious in the heart of man in all ages of history, and dramatically represented in the painful limping of Baudelaire's albatross and swan, penetrates and modifies every aspect of love. Time does not bring any solution to love, but it changes love. Baudelaire is not characterized solely by abulia and prevarication. If the absence of will power and the attraction of the lie inhabit Baudelaire, his work testifies to the strong will of the artist and to a purity of spirit which is one of the most beloved aspects of truth.

The darkness of Baudelaire is the same which enveloped Rimbaud, Lautréamont, Apollinaire, Cocteau—namely, the most purely tragic of the French poets. The concentrated point of their night, however, is a diamond, which is human suffering in a very pure state, and which is suitable to darkness, as the very pure joy of the saints is suitable to the fathomless light of God. The order of darkness. From the depths of this Baudelairian order which is in reality the microcosm of our corrupted heritage and of Eden's drama, the poet, in his *Fleurs du Mal*, revindicated an ancient tradition of the Catholic artist. He gave to his period the image of the Christian faith which his period deserved. Or rather the true image of the faith in his period. Owing to their universal faith, the Middle Ages created an art superior to the artist, an art which celebrates the dignity of man because man celebrates the glory of God as naturally as he breathes. But today's simplicity is not yesterday's. The Christian faith of today is fragmentary, wounded by the infidelity of a Calvin, of a Rousseau, of a Nietzsche. The modern artist no longer sees the transparency of the world, he sees its opaqueness. Modern man, no longer able to contemplate the glory of Christ resurrected, can look only on the agony of Christ crucified.

Thus Baudelaire founded, in spite of himself and because of his century, the school of darkness, as Jean Cocteau will represent in the twentieth century, in spite of his desire not to belong to any group, the school of the tight rope. Baudelaire's abyss, where light is inaccessible —where man in chains dreams and suffers; becomes Cocteau's circus where the illumination is artificial and where man runs about perpetually like a demon with his strange and comic gestures. But the stamp of the Catholic baptism explains both men: the man in chains, immobilized in the darkness, who was Baudelaire; and the clown, walking on his tight rope, exhibited in the cruel glare of the footlights and the side shows, who was Cocteau. Divine love could not penetrate Baudelaire's abyss, but the poet believed in it through his desire to believe in it.

Baudelaire sought and implored a less fragmentary faith, and the few rare moments when he believed he had attained it are among the most intensely pure in Christian poetry. The purity of a work ends always by triumphing, and time, which robs everything which passes with it, has consecrated the purity of the desire in Baudelaire and has equalled it for us today to the realization of desire. One does not desire without receiving some recompense. Even men can perceive this principle.

As for Dante, the sun was at times for Baudelaire the symbol of transposition and purification. But generally, in *Les Fleurs du Mal*, the sun recaptured its ancient meaning of phallic symbol, such as we have studied it in *Le Pitre Châtié* of Mallarmé and in *Phèdre* of Racine. Baudelaire's central drama is better explained by the confusion which existed in his mind between the symbolism of eternal life and of momentary physical life. The sun in *Les Fleurs du Mal* represents the same drama of destiny which it translates in *Phèdre*.

When the lyricism is intact and the verse stripped of all bombast, when a perfect equilibrium between experience and language is attained, as, for example in *Le Balcon*, the rôle of the sun reaffirms Baudelaire as the poet of human love. At the beginning of this remarkable poem, which is a synthesis of Baudelaire's drama and of his art, passion has just created a new being in the poet. But the poem, rather than describing passion, describes its absence. The spirit of the man, at first, seems reintegrated and purified after the drama of passion. The balcony is that moment of waiting and lassitude when the spirit can contemplate the heavens after having exhausted all the physical games. But the balcony isn't real. The lovers don't remain on it.

The night descends from the same heavens, and, enveloping the balcony, terminates the pure moment of contemplation. The 'soleils rajeunis' of the last stanza announce the same carnal experience which is being reborn, an experience whose death, at the beginning of the poem, had made possible the desire for purity. If the sun symbolizes the return of passion, which for Baudelaire designates the renewal of enslavement, the final stanza of *Le Balcon* contains an astonishingly sexual image. The spirit is therefore abandoned, and this great poem of Baudelaire gives us, after *Phèdre*, one of the purest portraits of the tragic.

Human love, according to *Les Fleurs du Mal*, is a tragedy both humble and ridiculous. Between *L'Albatros*, one of the first poems, and *Recueillement*, one of the last, the whole drama of Baudelaire is narrated. The drama didn't change during the poet's life. The distance covered between youth and old age, between the sea and the city, between the solitude of nature and the loneliness of the city, between totemism and the turbine, is in reality the distance between adolescent love (*L'Albatros*) where the hero is ridiculed as a castrated boy, and the man who speaks to his grief as to his small daughter engendered by him and who shows him the death of himself in the symbol (still phallic) of the sun which goes to sleep and in the night which moves (*Receuillement*).

Baudelaire loved this return to the night which he translated elsewhere in his work by the return to the earth, to the tomb, to the breast. All these words are synonymous with *abyss* and describe too often an Oedipus situation for us to explain Baudelaire's love in any other way. In his sonnet *Le Gouffre* he lists other synonyms, still more striking, of the word *abîme:* 'action, désir, rêve, Parole'! All these words which we might willingly have applied to other artists, Baudelaire reassembles in himself in order to name the great void of sleep and nightmare. The microcosm for Baudelaire is the matrix. Love is the bottomless maternal abyss.

The word 'action' evokes for us a Saint Bernard whose charity is love of man and love of God felt simultaneously.

'Désir' recalls to mind Plotinus and his detachment from the world, the flight toward the One, the waiting, and finally, the invasion and the possession of the One. 'Rêve' we associate with Nerval, who didn't use the mystical way of Plotinus, but who chose free association, chance, the gratuitous, the activity of the subconscious and even madness. And 'Parole', the last word in the Baudelairian list of synonyms, evokes the names of Blake, Hugo, Whitman, and all those writers whose memory of true Christianity was transformed into a pre-Christian religion. Hugo remained near to God, but he was not near to Christ and the New Law. The poetry of these artists of the 'word' is a cosmogonic song and a pantheistic prayer.

In his disquietude Baudelaire aspired to return to the Source, which he confused, subconsciously perhaps, with maternal love, with the depths of the ocean and the abyss. He remained the child in whom the meaning of evil was always translated by the image of a trap or of a black hole. Pascal's disquietude was nearer the Source, and that is why, perhaps, Baudelaire will always appear to us more comprehensible, more beloved, and more human.

4: *Masks of the Modern Hero*

THE VOYOU: VILLON, RIMBAUD, APOLLINAIRE
I

THE VOYOU LIVES in a world apart. He hardly ever passes the frontiers of a world which lies just beyond the world of bourgeois society. But he doesn't live there alone. The voyou has a brother who never remains very far away from him. This brother is called at times clown or acrobat or fool. Once he was called a juggler. He has even been called by the polite name of Harlequin. And from time to time fate lends him the pretentious name of poet.

The soul of a voyou is not improvised. Neither is it the simple mechanical result of a life of privation and of a sordid environment. The picturesque and choreographic aspect of the voyou touches us much less than his heart which may beat in a body stiffly conventional and nourished on succulent food. But the two species of voyou: the poor voyou, born among the people and spending his life at some distance from bourgeois comforts, and the rich voyou, born in the bourgeoisie and spending his life at some distance from the crowded and ill-famed dives of the real voyous, are both the taciturn man of society. The clown performs mute rites, as poetry always celebrates something silent, some wilfully silenced voice.

The silence of the voyou covers inner worlds. Both the voyou and the clown testify to a complicated agility, but the public before which they gesticulate and tumble never hears them speak. Their gestures are not accompanied by any verbal explanation. Their hearts are not exhibited at the same time as their supple bodies. And yet their hearts may contain the inalterable wisdom of human sorrow. The heart is never improvised as are the awkward and comic actions of the clown.

The greatest lyric poetry is adorned with this heart which is both admirable and fragile. It is admirable in its search for the absolute: the absolute of the gesture and its taciturn eloquence; it is fragile in the love to which it gives itself, because of all human sentiments love is the most mobile. Its future is the most uncertain and unstable of futures. There is something of the voyou and the terrified genius in Des Grieux and in Alceste, whom Manon and Célimène never allow to say all they have to say, all they would like to say, all that they were born to say, all that they don't cease saying during their death.

The voyou and his brother the clown teach us that true fantasy does not exist and that joy in its pure state is not human. All fantasy is composed of seriousness and all joy borders on sorrow. The voyou is the human being in whom the two worlds of joy and sorrow are confused. The Middle Ages was his great period when he moved about with more naturalness, because the inspiration of the clown, like that of the Middle Ages, is both solemn and naive.

Men are born voyous as others are born blind. An inexplicable fate seems to reign at the birth of men, and each life appears to be either privileged or damned. With this observation I do not believe I am contradicting the great dogma of freedom: the voyou remains free in his flight, as the banker remains free in his bank. Flight! the voyou is the man who escapes from everything that normally holds back other men: studies, family, civic duties, religious duties. The voyou is the adventurer of space, of non-passable roads, of the immense freedom of cities and fields.

II

At the birth of French poetry, there came into existence a first model of this clownish voyou, whom I like to consider founder of a long race of weak men who live outside of their real life and whose sole vigour is their poetry. I refer to a brief work of the end of the twelfth century, written in the language of the Ile-de-France. Its author is unknown, but the piety he put in his story and the sympathy he had for his hero prove to us that he understood the clown's vocation and the poet's vocation which are perhaps identical.

The title of this poèm, *Le Jongleur de Notre Dame*, reveals the paradox of this double vocation: the existence and the exercise of the juggler: that is, the man who amuses the public in the open air; and the other adventure of the same juggler which is that of piety. The juggler is the man of movement and dynamics. In leaving the open world of the street and the public square for the silent and closed world of the monastery, the juggler, or rather the 'tumbler' as he is called, discovers that his vocation of an acrobat is his one sanctification and the one reality of his life. The new love for God by which he wishes to live is inextricably bound up with his clown's tricks. He has to serve Our Lady in the one trade he knows. The purity of his intention—his dance will be a kind of prayer—converts a popular amusement into a religious celebration.

At night, in Our Lady's chapel, where he believes he is alone, he dances before the statue of the Virgin, and performs for her his hardest and most fatiguing tricks. All the juggler's agile and comic movements which formerly delighted or bored the holiday public, are now converted into a very pure act of adoration. This twelfth century juggler is a prefiguration of the fifteenth century poet, François Villon. Both knew a voyou's existence: the first was a clown-voyou, and the second a poet-voyou. And both existed for a public: the juggler for a mocking transitory public which he could hold only by the grotesque element of his dances; and Villon, for a public of voyou friends and criminals who heeded only the coarse and obscene parts of his 'ballades'.

They existed for a popular public of squares and taverns, but they both sought another public more fervent and more sure than the one they were accustomed to. The juggler sought a holy spectator before whom his most expert human actions would find grace. And this juggler had the miraculous experience of finding in his lifetime the public he sought. But Villon, like every true poet, sought a public whom he knew destined to be posthumous. The juggler's art disappeared with him: the creation

82

of a dance is in time and space; but Villon's art began to live after the poet's death, because poetry is an art situated just beyond time and space.

At the end of the adventure between the juggler and his divine public in whose honour he performed his most brilliant acrobatics, the Virgin dried with her veil the clown's sweat. The first drama of the voyou had a happy ending. The Virgin's gesture which was both human and miraculous proved the purity that had been conquered by the clown's heart.

At the final moment of our life we are judged in terms of our love, of the greatness of our love. This is the spiritual meaning of the twelfth century story: of the juggler's example and of his youthful virility. God's love consecrated the voyou's antics at the very moment when the voyou offered up his antics to God. The juggler of Notre Dame resembles Francis, the poor man of Assisi whose actions often remind us of prestidigitations, and Saint Julien l'Hospitalier in Flaubert's story, because Julien was another exile who first performed a monstrous kind of magic and then received the reward of Love. The juggler is therefore the being who leaves himself—like the poet in the deepest sense of his vocation. The clown and the poet are two men, very slightly limited by their bodies, who aspire to be invaded by God.

III

Villon was much more of a voyou than the juggler, and his entire life, as much of it as we know today, seems composed of a series of prestidigitations. His heart seems limitless when we consider the diverse rôles he played: martyr, lover, sinner, poverty-stricken criminal, hanged culprit, pious Catholic, voyou. Yet, there was a great unity in his heart which traversed all the natural and improvised rôles of this literary clown.

The first Villon, of the *Petit Testament*, was the abandoned lover, the martyr lover. The poet is twenty-four years old. It is winter, in Paris, where the wolves feed on the wind ('où les loups se vivent de vent') and where people stay inside ('où l'on se tient en sa maison'). Villon announces that he is going to leave:

Adieu, je m'en vais à Angers

and we remember that every departure of a poet is a flight. The poet and the voyou don't leave, as other men do, with a copy of *Life* and *The New Yorker* in their left hand, and a valise containing a tooth brush and a pair of pyjamas in their right hand. And even if the poet is somewhat bourgeois in appearance and leaves with a real valise, that mustn't count too much against him because it is only his heart which travels. The poet's departure is therefore a flight, an evasion, a seizure of the unreal. Villon tells us in this first picture of the *Petit Testament* that he leaves his heart to his mistress:

Je laisse mon coeur enchassé
Pâle, piteux, mort et transis

But the last Villon we know, of the *Grand Testament*, makes a different gift of his heart. Like the juggler who had offered to Notre Dame his art of acrobat and dancer, Villon, when he had attained his full and tragic knowledge of life, offers his heart to the same divine Mistress:

Je donne ma pauvre âme
A la benoîte Trinité,
Et la commande à Notre Dame,
Chambre de la divinité.

Both of these men: the juggler who was the poet of action, of suppleness, and of somersaults, and Villon who was the athlete of verses that sing and of 'ballades', were two adventurers of space who, after knowing all the physical frontiers, left spaces, roads, and cities in order to close themselves within a final freedom. The juggler left the wind and the rain of public squares for a chapel. Villon left the prisons, the taverns, and the whore houses for the very pure domain of poetry. 'Poésie est délivrance', François Mauriac wrote in his *Journal* (vol. 3, p. 185), and the formula is accurate if the poet surpasses himself in his work.

In their lives of voyou, the juggler and Villon knew themselves: the first necessary knowledge of a man is knowledge of himself. But the juggler, in his dance before

Our Lady, and Villon, in his poetry, attained a second form of knowledge, that of the universal self. Thus, the dream of life is seconded by the dream of what is eternal. Every work of art, whether it be the poetry of a ballade or the comic dance of a clown, testifies to a dualism of powers. Both natural and supernatural, these powers are at the immutable source of all poetry and all sacrificed life.

IV

Almost three centuries separate the juggler and Villon; three other centuries separate Villon and Rimbaud. In Rimbaud, the supreme voyou of modern poetry, we can see the same desire (or perhaps the same suffering) of playing multiple rôles and hiding behind multiple masks. Rimbaud describes himself: 'saltimbanque, mendiant, artiste, bandit, prêtre.' The ambition of changing one's life ('changer la vie') is the most insistent of adolescent ambitions. It is maintained, when the adolescent grows, especially in two types of men, the artist and the saint, because they are permanent adventurers by vocation and chivalrous knights in quest for what is unseizable, unreal, absurd. The ambition to change one's life controls the great lover of every age, a Saint Augustine, a Saint Bernard, and a Saint François de Sales as it controls the great voyou of every age—a Villon, pious voyou, and a Rimbaud, blasphemous voyou—who is incapable of being a lover, since he is destined to embrace suffering and always to leave the woman he might have loved.

The life of Rimbaud is an uninterrupted series of departures, and no poet, unless it is Baudelaire, has elaborated more than he on the theme of flight and evasion. At seven, in order to avoid his mother, a wilful and bigoted disciplinarian, young Arthur used to escape to the garden. This first flight of his first childhood prefigured the other flights in his life.

> Quand, lavé des odeurs du jour, le jardinet,
> Derrière la maison, en hiver, s'illunait:
> Gisant au pied d'un mur, enterré dans la marne
> Et pour visions écrasant son oeil darne,
> Il écoutait grouiller les galeux espaliers.

A few years later, the flight to the garden wall was not sufficient to satisfy the boy's restless soul. He undertook small flights to the Ardennes woods and the environs of Charleville. In a poem written at fifteen, he says:

> *Par les soirs bleus d'été, j'irai dans les sentiers . . .*
> *Et j'irai loin, bien loin, comme un bohémien.*

Rimbaud knew the life of a tramp and a vagabond, as Villon had known it, and like Villon also, he knew hunger and poverty. He begged along the roadside and at the doors of houses and barracks. Soon Paris attracted the adolescent, and then, in Verlaine's company, he visited Brussels, London, and Brussels again.

Verlaine was justified in calling him 'l'homme aux semelles de vent'. His ubiquity was amazing. Rimbaud stopped writing before his twentieth birthday. His literary work, composed between the ages of fifteen and nineteen, once completed, he was free to leave on his major voyages. 'L'homme aux semelles de vent' left France as if he was leaving a prison, for the warmer countries, for Abyssinia, for Java, for Italy. His ambulatory predilection required the vastest spaces and opened up to him the purest and most distant lands. The very first flight of the child, of the seven year old poet, to his mother's garden, was followed by a series of voyages which became increasingly exotic and ornate.

What interpretation can be given to this life of departures? What explication can we find in it for the brief literary work left by this voyou and consecrated in some way by the long silence which followed it?

In the first place, this life of pursuit and voyage was that of a vagabond, but it was also a poet's life, because poetry is born from physical and spiritual hunger. Whereas most men generally pursue multiple desires and multiple goals, the poet pursues his purity: what Rimbaud called his 'treasure' and which seems to us synonymous with 'innocency'. It is impossible for poets to waste time. Whatever they do, they cannot avoid accumulating in themselves the essence and the substance of a future poem. Whereas the pride of all his poses remains in the ordinary man in the state of sin and loss, in the poet it is transformed into a discipline and an exercise.

'La vraie vie est absente', said Rimbaud. He was the man predestined to departures and voyages, the adolescent predestined to leave Charleville and the banks of the Meuse, as Dante had to leave Florence and the banks of the Arno, as Hugo had to leave Paris to live on his island, as Hart Crane had to leave New York for Mexico, as Baudelaire had to leave imaginatively and embark upon the most spiritual and most solemn voyages of all the modern poets. *Exil* of St. John Perse is a recent poem, published in 1942, outside of France during the poet's exile, like a present day confirmation of that obscure hope which has always forced poets to abandon those who are known and dear to them.

And yet, at each step which the poets make in their predestined voyages, the same uneasiness overcomes them. Rimbaud, in Paris at the home of Verlaine, among the Parnassians, resembled the medieval juggler among the monks. Even there, in the midst of the representative and celebrated poets of the century, the real life for Rimbaud was absent. We think instinctively of Jesus among the doctors in the temple, and of the albatross of Baudelaire in the midst of the sailors who torture and mimic him. Rimbaud didn't stay among the Parnassians and he didn't remain lost for long among the occult dreams of the Orient. Everything is pretence for the poet: literary poses and metaphysical poses. Even the highest ambition which Rimbaud conceived, his messianic ambition, disappeared, and there only remained in him his desire to leave, which is the fatal desire of the voyou.

> Peut-être un Soir m'attend
> Où je boirai tranquille
> En quelque vieille Ville.

According to this lesson of the inevitable voyage, fated but never ending, we are able to understand that the poetic mind never learns anything. It knows all in advance: it is the spirit of all humanity, of the past and of the future. Rimbaud was the voyou guide. He was almost the mystical guide, to the same degree that Villon was the guided mystic. But Rimbaud, more disconcerted than Villon, was less Christian.

Rimbaud was so profoundly a poet that we become more and more unknowing spectators of his work. His personal struggle was so much larger than his work, that his readers are perforce strangers to the conflict.

Rimbaud's personal debate was another form of flight in which he spared himself no suffering. After all the physical and real flights, Rimbaud undertook his real poet's flight which was his flight before the ordinary locutions of language, before all familiar words, and even before the memory of language. He was the 'voyant', and at the same time the mystic, the messiah of the new poetic alchemy. 'Je notais l'inexprimable', he wrote in *Une Saison en Enfer*. 'Je fixais des vertiges.' The poet not only sought a poetic language worthy of bearing his experience, he explored the universe of his heart for the transcendental language for the poetry which would celebrate the silent and untranslatable message of his heart. The attempt was not pursued for very long. It has been recommended in our day by James Joyce who, perhaps because he didn't feel the same torture of the absolute that Rimbaud did, was successful in creating a new language. On three levels Rimbaud failed in his search: on the physical level first: his adventure of traveller, in stations and harbours, never brought him peace; on the literary level, next: his poems and his prose, incapable of reflecting the full light of his genius, were always considered by him artistic failures; and lastly, on the metaphysical level : his verbal acrobatics did not win the grace and salvation which the juggler's acrobatics did.

V

Apollinaire is another of the many-masked voyou poets who traverse life in search for their climate. Great poets are inexplicable in terms of normal and natural geography. Like Villon and Rimbaud, Apollinaire spent time in prison. In 1911, the celebrated *Mona Lisa* of Da Vinci disappeared from the Louvre. Guillaume Apollinaire was arrested on the seventh of September and sent to the

Prison de la Santé, from which he was released on the twelfth.

In time, every major poet becomes legendary. Even before their death, Villon and Rimbaud had disappeared from the ordinary life of men, and legends were already converting the features of their faces and the expressions of their souls into features and expressions of mythic and unknown men. But Guillaume Apollinaire during his real existence, immediately, appeared as a legendary character. He was born legendary, he didn't become so. Mystery surrounded him from birth. He was both a Polish aristocrat because he bore the name Wilhelm-Apollinaris de Kostrowitski, and a French poet because he also bore the name Guillaume Apollinaire. One of his best friends, Pablo Picasso, rather than painting him as a gentleman or as a poet, made a portrait of him dressed in a bishop's robe as if he were a Roman prelate, with a mitre on his head and a pastoral ring on his finger.

After two major poets: Villon, poet of death, and Rimbaud, poet of life, we come to Apollinaire who is a poet of life and death. In a sense, he closes the series of voyou poets because his spiritual affinities lie not so much with Rimbaud and Villon, as with the simple juggler of the twelfth century. Apollinaire, like the juggler of Notre Dame, is innocent and naive. He represents more simplicity in his poet's vocation, as the juggler represented the greatest simplicity in his clown's trade. All of these poets exalted the primitive being in themselves, the juggler poet as well as the real poets. They all sought their own identity because they wished to trick the fate of tragedy. Villon and Rimbaud, with an indescribable anguish; the juggler and Apollinaire, with much simplicity and even light-heartedness, all tried to become who they were.

In spite of the briefness of Apollinaire's life, as brief as Villon's and Rimbaud's, and in spite of all the colours of legends with which it has been abundantly disguised, it appears to us today much less tormented than Villon's and Rimbaud's, less guided by prayer than Villon's life, less consecrated to the search of purity than Rimbaud's life. I know that there are many undiscovered details in the lives of these three artists, and it is possible that we lack the most important facts to understand their drama and their personal psychology. Their poetry, when all is said, is only the vestige of some vaster and more comprehensible drama of man. In poetry we are offered only the reflection of fires.

The child and the poet spend their richest hours in the realm of the imagination. But the imagination of a child is autonomous, so to speak, without responsibility, fairylike, whereas the imagination of the artist is charged with all the meaning of life. In the heart of this being whom we have taken on the strange custom of calling clown or voyou or pilgrim, his imagination exists thanks to an immense courage. The courage of his imagination is the temporal and spiritual measurement of every artist. With a Pascal, this courage is perhaps reason, the geometrical spirit which is closely associated with the sensitivity of his heart: with a Rimbaud it was perhaps his flight through all the possible landscapes in search for Eden's purity; with a Guillaume Apollinaire it was a temperate and tender questioning of the universe, a true kyriel of childish questions which, in full innocency, sounded the gravest mysteries.

A poor traveller like Villon and Rimbaud, Apollinaire was the new type of errant ghost in the twentieth century. He was the emigrant. Born in Rome, he spent his youth in Provence. He travelled through Germany, Bohemia, Holland, but always preferred Paris. There he lived the longest, in the Paris of fogs and masked faces, surrounded by friends. He always needed a great many friends. For them, Apollinaire was the charitable and kindly man who laughed very loud, whose smile was affectionate but enigmatical, and whose apartment, a bizarre apartment in the Boulevard Saint-Germain, contained some beautiful Picassos, a Marie Laurencin, and a Chirico. In any profound sense, he was unknown to his friends, but he was celebrated for his boldness and his sense of the new. Without being a leader, he had a marked influence over men. For his friends, he was also the man who loved an uproar and who was able to live in it. At the first performance of his play, *Les Mamelles de Tirésias*, the curtain had to be lowered because of the hisses and hoots of the public. Philippe Soupault, who was prompter, tells how he saw Apollinaire appear proud and joyful, shouting with all his might: 'cochons, cochons!' He was celebrated not only for his long walks through the countryside, but also for gastronomical knowledge. Gourmandizing was an important trait of his legendary character. He loved everything: snails, petits fours, cucumbers. He loved everything except red meat and British cooking.

Compared with the miraculous poetry of Villon and Rimbaud, Guillaume Apollinaire's work appears like a reflection of great poetry. But the reflection is obsessive and subtle. Apollinaire has already taken his place among those men who will not leave us, whose numerous and tragic departures in life, whose instability and restlessness have immobilized them for us and for the future spiritual life of men.

Deliberately, Apollinaire recaptured the rhythm and the formulas of Villon. It was in homage to the first great poet of France that he recalled the ancient melancholy of the ballades.

> *Où sont-ils Braque et Max Jacob*
> *Derain aux yeux gris comme l'aube*
> (*Calligrammes*, p. 76.)

Like T. S. Eliot who has reproduced many lines of Jules Laforgue in giving them a new colour, Apollinaire refashioned the folk lyricism of Villon, of Nerval, and of Verlaine, a lyricism composed of unanswered questions and silenced stories which provoke a tender and suggestive nostalgia:

> *Où sont-ils ces beaux militaries*
> *Soldats passés Où sont les guerres*
> *Où sont les guerres d'autrefois*
> (*ibid., p.* 85.)

Apollinaire encouraged both in his life and in his poetic composition a kind of chance. Gratuitous images spring up in his verses like natural reflexes and spontaneous answers to the subconscious law of chance and free association. The most familiar objects and the most trivial scenes become purified in his writing. His image of the window, for example, seems to be almost a new procedure in poetic experience:

> *La fenêtre s'ouvre comme une orange*
> *Le beau fruit de la lumière.*
>
> (*Calligrammes, p.* 17.)

The principle of deciphering the meaning of things, which was the principle of Baudelaire's aesthetics, is abandoned by Apollinaire for the freedom and the fecundation of the subconscious.

In his long poem, *La Chanson du Mal-Aimé*, Apollinaire found not only his most chaste accents—no poetry is more chaste except perhaps a few stanzas of Baudelaire in *L'Invitation au Voyage* and *Moesta et Errabunda*—but he discovered his most significant mask, his most individualized rôle. In Villon we saw the prisoner and the exile, in Rimbaud the voyou and the traveller, and now in Apollinaire we see, above all, the mask of the 'mal-aimé', that is of the rejected lover, faintly reminiscent of the 'amant martyr' in Villon. The personal story and the universal theme are mingled in this subtle song of Apollinaire, as the soul and the body are mingled in Pascalian psychology. We are told that the inspirer of the poem was Marie Laurencin, but the facts are as vaguely defined in it as in the most anonymous of folk songs. Love is not evoked in it, but the past of a love which has never lived:

> *Comment faire pour être heureux*
> *Comme un petit enfant candide*
>
> (*Alcools, p.* 27.)

The voyou who appears at the beginning of the piece:

> *Un soir de demi-brume à Londres*
> *Un voyou qui ressemblait à*
> *Mon amour vint à ma rencontre*
> *Et le regard qu'il me jeta*
> *Me fit baisser les yeux de honte*

is perhaps the poet's double because the voyou is the supreme being of silence whose experiences are never related explicitly with the logic of royal experiences. The voyou and the clown abolish the truth of their words and flee the reality of their adventures and their cities.

The persistent vision of Guillaume Apollinaire in the

company of painters, recalls other visions: of the juggler in the midst of the monks, of Villon among the criminals, and of Rimbaud among the Parnassians. All these men knew the same danger, which is that of the acrobat, of falling into the public which looks at them. The word 'cubism' was pronounced for the first time by Henri Matisse as he was examining some canvasses brought up from the south of France by Georges Braque. Apollinaire became the interpreter of cubism and is likewise prominent at the beginning of the dadaist and surrealist movements. If the juggler, Villon, and Rimbaud always resisted the various groups in the midst of which they lived, Apollinaire, on the contrary, was more easily assimilated with the painters, and especially with the three painters who were closest to him: Picasso, Braque, and Marie Laurencin. Picasso's art engendered not only an aesthetics but a metaphysics as well, and, in a certain sense, the pristine greatness of the poet Apollinaire is mysteriously hidden in the paintings of the Malaguena Picasso.

Whereas Picasso questions the universe severely, Apollinaire questions it timidly, with tenderness and nostalgia. The poet defined painting with these words: 'An astonishing art whose light is limitless' ('un art étonnant et dont la lumière est sans limites.') But this unapproachable liberty of light which is at the source of the great geniuses in painting, does not exist for poets. They do not work with light, but with suffering, and this very suffering which provides Apollinaire with his most chaste and most melancholy accents, makes Picasso all the more severe. Picasso and Apollinaire never leave their worshipped pantheisms, but the struggle between man and his pantheism (or the struggle between man and his universe) is more ferocious and more tragic in the painter Picasso than in the poet Apollinaire.

VI

The harlequins of Picasso who often in his paintings accompany women and men, but without resembling either the women or the men, belong to the species of voyous as well as to the species of clowns. The harlequins of Picasso, the tumblers (saltimbanques) of Apollinaire, and the voyou who Rimbaud was, are all the same man whom we like to consider the representative type of modern hero. He is the disarmed heart in the midst of cruel brothers. He knows, as profoundly as the other men who cannot understand him, that love is the sole richness. He is the man who will occupy a place in the prayers of men (when they don't want to be troubled by him), he is the one whom other men will never lose but whom they will never love.

Human life of the earth is never over—this is the most relentless principle in our existence—and only the work of art, in the life of men, can be terminated. The voyou, more than all other men, is the most incomplete and the most solitary, but he has revindicated his rights in modern art where he has attained a unity of tragic attitude and spiritual fervour that other literary heroes do not possess. The voyou is not only the clown of modern heroes, he is their angel, the only angel perhaps today who lives among men. Painters, for lack of real angels in their imagination, have replaced them by clowns, and Watteau's *Gilles* counts innumerable brothers on the canvasses of Picasso, of Cézanne, and of Rouault. Musicians like Erik Satie and Stravinsky have composed their best music for clowns. And poets, finally, have been reincarnated countless times in the clown who lives by some mysterious principle of angelism.

Apollinaire died on the day of the armistice 1918, not having finished the order of his adventure which was, by its very character, limitless.

> *Pitié pour nous qui combattons toujours aux frontières*
> *De l'illimité et de l'avenir.*
>
> *(Calligrammes, p. 220).*

This was approximately the same year when Hart Crane, the voyou-angel and the Rimbaud of New York, spoke in his poem *Legend* of living in life and living at the same time outside of life. Hart Crane was the angel who was both voyou and man, the clown who had to believe in the

94

phantoms he incarnated, as Narcissus had to believe in himself in the reflections of the mirror:

> *Twice and twice*
> *(Again the smoking souvenir,*
> *Bleeding eidolon!) and yet again.*
> *Until the bright logic is won*
> *Unwhispering as a mirror*
> *Is believed.*

> *(Collected Poems, p.* 61)

A few years later, in 1921, another American poet, T. S. Eliot, in *The Hollow Men*, described the same tragic existence of the clown, whose body, like Petrouchka's, is stuffed with straw, and whose soul, like the soul of Villon's hanged criminals, is tormented.

> *Remember us—if at all—not as lost*
> *Violent souls, but only*
> *As the hollow men*
> *The stuffed men.*

> (T. S. Eliot, *The Hollow Men*)

This was the same period when, in Paris, Jean Cocteau peopled his poetry with angels and his plays with sad gigolos who also belong to the race of clowns. It was at this time that Charlie Chaplin symbolized modern man for the French artists, Charlie Chaplin whom Marc Chagall drew bearing his head in one hand and an angel's wing under his left arm. Mistinguet, in a certain sense, was Charlie Chaplin for Paris. Countless times she played the rôle of voyou on the stage of the Casino de Paris and the Folies Bergères, the same rôle which Chaplin played on the screen and which the acrobats played in the Cirque Médrano. 'Chaplin, c'est le guignol moderne', wrote Jean Cocteau who knew so intensely that the clowns throw us all of life compressed. Cocteau, who was more a prey to angelism than most modern artists, has written one of the most astonishing sentences of modern criticism. It is a sentence hidden away in a small note at the bottom of one of his pages: 'Rimbaud and Mallarmé have become our Adam and Eve. The apple is Cézanne's. We shall always bear the weight of original sin.' ('Rimbaud, Mallarmé sont devenus notre Adam et Eve. La pomme est de Cézanne. Nous porterons toujours le poids du péché originel.' *Le Rappel à l'Ordre*, p. 183.)

For each of these portraits, beginning with the juggler of Notre Dame and ending with Guillaume Apollinaire, I have had the impression of drawing the same sketch. They are figures of different sizes, but all represent the same model. They have the same heart of an exile which in each age, has clung on to so little. Villon speaks of this in his *Débat*:

Ton coeur
Ne tient plus qu'à un petit filet.

The poet's heart, which beats so feebly in the world, has fear and need of hearing itself, as Narcissus, leaning over the water has fear and need of seeing himself. In both cases, the poet's heart which hears itself and Narcissus who looks at himself, make strange couples. They are two kinds of Narcissus: he who is psychologically so by nature, and he who is fatally so by necessity.

Each man, even the voyou whose heart continues to live without daring to love and who bends down to look at the hidden secret of his life, is irreplaceable. Human dignity resides in the most imperfect human nature provided it is struggling. Evil and grace both besiege man. The voyou moves us by the blackmail with which the world makes him cower. He is not the poet of images, but the poet for whom the meaning of images counts. As an angel is often the ambassador of God to men and the intercessor between the saints and men, the voyou is the intercessor between men and the void, between the rich heart of happy men and the void where the heart ceases to beat.

THE ARTIST: PROUST AND JOYCE

I

Any consideration of Proust and Joyce gives rise immediately to an important problem, that of the artist: his life, his function, his *raison d'être*, his suffering, the force of his spirit, his attitude toward his period, toward his work, toward his heart. Since the Renaissance, this has been a constant intellectual problem, but no period has examined it with more ardour and piety than our own. The works of Proust and Joyce are known today especially by writers and artists. But students in the universities are also beginning to read them, and their public is growing. They are being accepted more and more universally as artists, as geniuses, as perhaps the greatest of their time.

Each new reading of Proust or Joyce permits a deeper understanding of the mystery of a creative artist's sensitivity; or rather a clearer difference between the genius of an artist and the genius of a great artist. And yet it is very difficult to articulate in words and to define with precision with what elements is formed the art of a Proust or of a Joyce. The work of each evokes a world. Proust evokes Paris: its boulevards and its salons, and a few villages near Paris: their gardens, their rivers, their church spires. Joyce evokes Dublin: its streets and its pubs; and the outskirts of Dublin: Phœnix Park, the Liffey River. Each novelist is anchored in his own city: the horizon of Paris and the horizon of Dublin stretch beyond their limits without changing their name. A single city mysteriously becomes a universe. Not a single city alone—but a single salon, a single tavern becomes an inhabited universe, abundant and autonomous. This is the first triumph of a great artist: the creation of a very particularized world and period as that of *Ulysses'* twenty-four hours or as that of the night in *Finnegans Wake*.

This would not be sufficient, however. The Paris created by Proust and the Dublin created by Joyce are not sufficient guarantee to dub them 'artists'. Even the Paris and Dublin simultaneously so geographical and universal of these two literary works. It is necessary for the artist to reveal another universe, more impalpable than the first, more invisible, but quite as authentic. I mean the universe of the heart, the ancient world of the human spirit. The Frenchman and the Irishman of the twentieth century, whose art will be the subject of this study, not only knew their hearts, but possessed hearts rich in experience, in intuition, and in suffering. This heart is the true site of the work. Here we are touching on the only possible meaning of that troublesome word 'realism'. The only valid realism is the heart's, the realism of Saint Augustine, Dante, Pascal, Proust, Joyce.

The two works under consideration here are long and difficult. We believe this another trait of the great artist. What is particularly moving in a study of Proust and Joyce is their untiring vigour and recommencing of thought, the endurance of the creative mind and its intelligence. If we are moved by the beauty of the work, its multiple operations, its richness and courage, the two artists were moved by their material. This breaks out at each page. Their material is language. Their religion is language. Their symbol, myth, cosmos, and infinity are language. They are two artists of the word and of the sentence, two renovators, hierophants of the consecration of language. The spiritual life of the work has in some way replaced the spiritual life of the artist. The exaltation felt by Proust and Joyce in the mystery and power of their material which is language, was not felt in the same degree by other artists of the word, such as Dante, Milton, Racine. The great writer, in all centuries before ours, imposed limitations on language by his subject, sensitivity, and knowledge. He reduced language and forced it to bend to the exigencies of his thought. But Proust and Joyce discovered in language a limitless force and inexhaustible symbolism. Language, for them is more powerful than thought, and richer than the personal experience of any one man.

The work of Proust and Joyce, therefore, gives us an experience of renovation. This dual work doubtless marks a new stage in the history of the novel. In any case it represents two vast testaments of the modern novel, and two literary efforts written in an opulent language which does not possess a terminal character. The genius of Proust and Joyce is not only that of the novelist, it is also the lyric genius which creates a song, the genius which is not tricked by that abortion which time is endlessly seeking to effect in us.

Proust and Joyce both began their careers with a volume

of stories. *Les plaisirs et les jours* of Proust and *Dubliners* of Joyce announce future themes in the more important subsequent work. The sixteen long volumes which make up Proust's one novel, *A la recherche du temps perdu*, have a solid musical architecture whose unity and unfolding become apparent to a reader attentive to the internal and external order of the work. The three novels of Joyce: *Portrait of the artist as a young man, Ulysses, Finnegans Wake*, each of which is longer and denser and more symbolic than the preceding novel, also represent a single work whose logic and development appear today unequivocably clear. *Du Côté de chez Swann* shows us Proust as a child; *A l'ombre des jeunes filles en fleur*, as an adolescent; *Albertine disparue*, as a lover; and finally, the last part, *Le temps retrouvé*, as an artist. It is precisely as an artist that James Joyce describes himself in his first novel, *Portrait of the artist as a young man.* The hero of Joyce's second novel, *Ulysses*, is the portrait of an ordinary man, and Earwicker, in the third novel, who appears under many masks and names, designates all of humanity, that is to say, all men who are in each man.

Thus, if we place side by side these two vast works, we perceive that Joyce's work follows Proust's and completes it. When joined, the two works narrate a long story whose initial part is the cycle of the child growing up to become an artist, and whose second part is the cycle of the artist passing through three phases of existence. He considers himself first, in Stephen; then he considers himself as the ordinary man, in Ulysses; and finally, in the somnolent Earwicker, he considers the meaning and complications of all humanity. The work of Proust is a novel of personalities and of a society. The work of Joyce is a series of three novels of personalities and of humanity. But the artist is behind each work, and each work performs a rite. 'Le monologue intérieur', or the stream of consciousness, thanks to its fecundity, is as inexhaustible as the taste of a 'madeleine' dipped in an infusion of linden tea. The two works of Proust and Joyce, united together, represent, by the magnitude of their enterprise, the most recent attempt in the domain of literature to solve the enigma of human happiness.

'Les vrais paradis sont les paradis qu'on a perdus', says Proust in *Le temps retrouvé*. I like to consider this sentence a kind of definition of the novel, especially applicable to the genesis and explanation of Proust's novel. This lost paradise becomes real in the created work. The artist liberates in his work the permanent and habitually hidden essence of things: a spoon touching a plate, the unevenness of the pavement in the Guermantes' courtyard, the church at Combray, the beach at Balbec. In literary composition the past is always trampling out the present, and what re-lives is the ancient and dead day. A novel is, so to speak, an act of love and of fidelity. The impressions which an artist attempts to fix are born in a space stretching out before him, made of pure matter, entirely distinct from the common things we see and touch. The life one resuscitates and re-creates in a work thus becomes the only real life. Doesn't Proust say: 'L'artiste qui renonce à une heure de travail pour une heure de causerie avec un ami sait qu'il sacrifie une réalité pour quelque chose qui n'existe pas'?

The paradise one loses may be the light one fears. A lost paradise is the negation of paradise; it is hell. Proust's novel has the scope of Dante's *Inferno* without possessing the knowledge or the consciousness of hell's law. A theologian of the Middle Ages, explaining the anagogical meaning of the title *A la recherche du temps perdu* would call it *A la recherche du paradis perdu*. In the life of men one cannot immobilize time, and in the life of angels one cannot immobilize paradise. Time is our domain of suffering as paradise is the domain of joy.

A work will always remain more profound than the man who composed it; Proust certainly didn't comprehend the extent of his book. He knew neither its secret existence nor the long roots of his thought. The primal earth of roots is hidden. A possible variation of Proust's striking formula: 'une heure n'est pas qu'une heure' would be 'une œuvre n'est pas qu'une œuvre'. A work may be the consciousness of an entire period and the subterranean renovation of life. As Dante descends the circles of his hell, the décor constantly changes. The Proustian circles change also, but the two works, the *Inferno* of the Middle Ages and the hell of the twentieth century, which is Proust's novel, are both static. Time is recaptured in them only to be immobilized. Artists fear the light which is in them and they do not always know the roots of their work. The loss of happiness for Proust, the absence of God in all his work, the static quality and sombre texture of the world he creates are characteristics of hell and the negation of the good. Proust's heart is like a cell of flames.

If Proust's work is reminiscent of Dante's *Inferno*, James Joyce's work, and notably *Finnegans Wake*, is reminiscent of the *Purgatorio*. Both Dante and Joyce had produced a youthful work which prophetically announced their future writing. On the last page of the *Vita Nuova* and on the last page of the *Portrait*, there is a sentence which explicates the still unwritten work destined to be the major production in the case of both writers. With the last sentence of the *Vita Nuova:* 'Spero di dire di lei quello che mai non fu detto d'alcuna', Dante states that he is to write of Beatrice what has never been written of a woman, and therein announced his poem, the *Divine Comedy*. In the last sentence of the *Portrait:* 'I go forth to encounter for the millionth time the reality of experience and to forge in the smithy of my soul the uncreated conscience of my race', Joyce, through his hero Stephen, analyses the meaning of his ultimate book, *Finnegans Wake*.

Of the three parts of Dante's poem, *Il Purgatorio* is closest to the modern spirit. It is the domain of flux, change, progression; it is the domain from which hope is not excluded and which is not the realm of beatitude. *Finnegans Wake* is the modern purgatory without the concept of progress. Giambattista Vico, the Italian philosopher of the end of the seventeenth century is the master mainly responsible for the conception of *Finnegans Wake* and its purgatory without progress, as Saint Thomas Aquinas is the philosopher mainly responsible for Dante's conception of purgatory based upon the concept of progress. *Ulysses* also is a book which does not conclude. Certain scenes, like that of the Public House, which is described during two hundred pages, preserves the characteristics of a purgatorial nightmare and hallucination. The hero is no longer Stephen, the young man of the preceding book who discovered in himself symptoms of an artist's vocation—it is Leopold Bloom, Jew, the most representative man or symbol of modern society, with his perpetual ferment and agitation. Like Homer's Odysseus, Bloom travels through a world, the world of a single day in Dublin. In *Finnegans Wake* the theme of ceaseless mobility is projected especially through the language developed by Joyce. This language changes and re-creates itself as human suffering does.

III

We ask the hero of an epic, of a tragedy, and of a novel to undergo a destiny or at least to reveal a destiny. Proust and Joyce have both created a hero, who appears to be a kind of triptych hero. For Proust it is the triptych: Swann, Charlus, and Marcel himself; and for Joyce it is the triptych: Stephen, Bloom, and Earwicker. In each instance, the last character subsumes the others: Marcel contains in himself Swann and Charlus, and H. C. Earwicker, whose initials designate the formula '*H*ere *C*omes *E*verybody', is, in effect, all men. Is there a leading trait in these modern heroes? What distinguishes these two triptychs of heroes from other literary heroes?

In the sixteenth and final volume of *A la recherche du temps perdu* Marcel finds himself alone in the Guermantes' library. He takes a book, turns its pages, and comes upon a passage which his mother read him when he was a child. Gradually, in the long dense pages of this final volume, he explains the genesis of the work. It is the work of a single man and a single sensitivity. His hero underwent the experience of the modern world without knowing action.

We have described the work of Proust and Joyce as the most recent attempt to solve the enigma of happiness. Proust's hero, when he recognizes himself as an artist at the end of the book states in a lengthy analysis his impotency to realize himself in any physical employment, in any effective action. Incapable of knowing the pleasure of love, he must always assimilate something with the pleasure of love, such as the sound of music or the beauty of a painting. Proust's hero is the hero of memory. Hamlet was also. But Hamlet was so naive with his memory that a modern hero may well feel embarrassment for him. The resurrection of memory are the great scenes of Proust's novel: the vision of the steeples of Martinville, the taste of the madeleine, the red mysterious appeal of Vinteuil's septet. The hero's one activity is the deciphering of his memory resurrection. Hamlet, the distant ancestor of Marcel, was incapable of deciphering his memory and the tragedy of Shakespeare is a failure in terms of psychological analysis. But Hamlet was not an artist and the modern hero has become one. Hamlet was not a scapegoat, the allegorical symbol in art, as Christ was for the Middle Ages; but the modern artist, because he is the hero of his books, has become the scapegoat. Hamlet, without any doubt, experienced all the sensations which the Proustian hero describes. We are not free to chose our sensations: they are inevitable and fortuitous. Whereas *Hamlet* is solely a work of 'sensations', Proust's novel is first a work of sensations, and secondly, a work in which the artist's intelligence operates on his sensations.

Art has become today an austere school, markedly more austere than it was during the Renaissance, and the novel has become progressively more difficult to read. But it is too easy to forget that the artist is not free in the creation of his art. He does not execute it as he would like. His art is necessary and hidden; he must discover it as the scientist has to discover a law of nature. The artist's sensitivity is so real a substance that he has only to look at it in order to re-create it. Proust's novel extends between two nights: the night in childhood when Marcel contemplates for the first time, in his small room at Combray, the volume of George Sand, *François le Champi*, perhaps the sweetest and saddest night of his life, when he had obtained from his parents a first abdication whence he could date the decline of his health and his will power;

and the evening when he contemplates in the Guermantes' library the same volume of George Sand and when he discovers that the purpose of his life is intimately associated with the purpose of art. Dante's hell created by the medieval Christian imagination has become with Proust the hell of modern subjectivism. Like the heroes of the Dantesque hell, the heroes of Proust are rooted in their vices which are their personality. The domain of personality is the new hell created by the modern spirit.

But in the last novel of Joyce, the purgatorial aspect is more striking than the infernal. Purgatory is a transition. Nothing is stabilized there. *Finnegans Wake* is written in a purgatorial language in which everything changes ceaselessly. Formulas are familiar but deformed. The priest's invocation: 'In the name of the Father, the Son, and the Holy Ghost' becomes in the new language of the new purgatory: 'In the name of the former and of the latter and their holocaust'; the cry of Saint Augustine 'O felix culpa' becomes 'O phœnix culprit'. But the meaning is clear because Phœnix Park in Dublin is constantly referred to in the book as Eden. The hero of the book, H. C. Earwicker, is confused with innumerable other heroes: Adam, Abraham, Noah, Humpty Dumpty, Napoleon, the archangel Michael, Saint Patrick, Jesse James. The heroine in the novel, who is Earwicker's counterpart, is the small river, Anna Liffey, or in Joyce's language, Anna Livia, who appears under more than four hundred names of rivers. Anna Livia represents Eve, Sarah, Isolde, Josephine, and (America is not forgotten!) Aimée Semple MacPherson.

Earwicker, with all his names, incarnations, heroes, and periods, is the hero of night, the hero who lives through all the meanings of all experiences. But this hero does not leave his purgatory. He is incarcerated in time, and in the flux of time, like some scapegoat unable to leave its desert. But at the end of the book, when dawn is rising and when Earwicker is to wake up, we know that this is a rebeginning in order to prepare another night. For Vico, as for James Joyce, civilization resembles the phœnix who rises from its own ashes only to perish afterwards. Joyce's cosmos is Phœnix Park.

With Proust, we are present at the passing of years, at changes, and at the reconstruction of everything in the creative mind and in the work. Proust's hero who watches himself without pity and who confesses he knew everything in advance, is truly the hero in connivance with his public beside whom Hamlet seems naive. Joyce's hero, who is all men, loses his identity; he is at once hero and public for himself. This no longer equates Proust's psychological analysis—it is a cosmological synthesis. It is not even the analysis of the subconscious, as it was in Proust; it is, in the last two books of Joyce, and especially *Finnegans Wake*, the poetry of Time which nothing retains and which nothing terminates.

Often in the *Divine Comedy* a single verse is sufficient for Dante to describe some character in some unforgettable attitude. We are thinking of Farinata degli Uberti, erect in his burning sepulchre as he appears in the sixth infernal circle of heresy:

> *ed el s'ergea col petto e con la fronte*
> *com'avesse l'inferno in gran dispitto.*

Farinata, his chest and head in a violent posture, as if he held in deepest scorn his torture, is an apparition of wild grandeur and beauty. The characters of Proust and Joyce also appear in burning sepulchres: their vices and their weaknesses take on an histrionic defiance. The artist of all periods likes this duplication of himself. He sees himself both as a young hero and as a mature man. Dante is first the traveller, and then he is Farinata whose pride maintains a sinister power in the midst of his flaming tomb. Rabelais has an obvious affection for his young Gargantua and a respect for his venerable Grandgousier. Shakespeare is himself not only in Hamlet but in Lear as well . . . Proust duplicates himself in Charlus who, like Farinata, remains haughty in his degradation and sin. And finally Joyce, who appears first as young Stephen, transforms himself into Bloom and Earwicker. Between the artist and his creation, as between his young hero and his mature hero, there exists a virile and abstract affection. It would not be

105

unjust to say that the mystery of creation resembles the mystery of paternity. And literary creation preserves the imprint of this mystery. It is Hamlet in search of his father's ghost, it is Telemachus in search of Odysseus, it is Marcel in search of Charlus, it is Stephen in search of Bloom. As in Pirandello's play, *Sei personaggi in cerca d'autore*, it is the character in search of his author, it is man in search of the artist in himself, and, in the final anagogical meaning, it is man in search of God. This profound principle of paternity and identification which penetrates the writing of Proust and Joyce joins them with the great creative minds of the past. Proust's hero is the individual man of the Renaissance: *A la recherche du temps perdu* is the modern epic of *Hamlet*; Joyce's hero is the universal man of the Middle Ages: *Finnegans Wake* is the modern version of *Il Purgatorio*.

IV

The meaning of a novel and of any work of art is intimately bound up with its fate. During the two major centuries of its history, the eighteenth and the nineteenth, the novel proved itself to be that form of art the nearest to life, the most capable of bearing life, the most free to reproduce the richness, complexity, and animation of life. Historical novels, analytical novels, realistic novels, naturalistic novels, *romans-fleuve*: each form tried to seize and channel life in its own way. All the manifestos, all the genres, all the schools, and all the best examples have culminated in this new form developed and elaborated by Proust and Joyce: the stream of consciousness novel. Its conception is grandiose, architectonic, and profound, but it appears today as the form of novel most surely destined to survive. Our contention in making this statement is that the novels of Proust and Joyce, more than all other novels, are symbols, and the most permanent principle of all art seems to us to be the inevitable necessity of creating a symbol.

A la recherche du temps perdu and *Finnegans Wake* are resisting symbols created by a harsh necessity, and represent two triumphs of modern art. A symbol is the expression of a human experience whose total meaning escapes the comprehension both of the man who created it and the man who contemplates it. Who can say that he understands completely the meaning of Bach's B minor Mass, of the Sainte Chapelle, or of a Cézanne landscape?

Proust's novel is the survival of all the sorrow dammed up within himself. The grief of his personal experience is the seed from which the work, which he composes later, is the plant. The symbol is therefore a visible and cruel beauty; visible because it appears in a form, and cruel because it exhibits for ever the grief of a human being. The work always testifies to a decantation which has taken place and to a kind of appeasement in the life of the artist. He writes when he is unfaithful to his suffering. His work is a posthumous infidelity. The artist thus accomplishes the first profanation of his memory, and afterwards, each reader accomplishes another. Each time we look at a painting of Picasso, we deform it and violate it. The picture itself is changed every day by the violations of all the eyes which look at it. Proust has described this phenomenon in his sentence: 'Un livre est un grand cimetière où sur la plupart des tombes on ne peut plus lire les noms effacés'. A work which is not a symbol is quickly consumed and destroyed by this daily abuse it is submitted to. But a pure work, which is a symbol, is protected by its profundity and forbids its own creator, and other men and artists, to rid themselves of its deep layers of universal and personal meanings. The symbol is invincible. It is a sentinel clement before contemplation, but inflexible before attack. The fate of the novel is therefore bound up with its conception of the symbol. The symbol is the measure of experience, richer and truer than experience. All the suffering of experience finds in it its value, its conscience, and its reality.

A great book is infallibly a book of love. Whether it be the *Song of Songs*, the *Enneads* of Plotinus, the sonnets of Shakespeare, *Phèdre*, or *Les Fleurs du Mal*, each great page of literature touches directly or indirectly on the central problem of human life. In Marcel's love for his grandmother and in Earwicker's love for his sons, thanks to the hard symbol of these two experiences capable of revealing the force of every love experience, we feel the unity and greatness of the work as clearly as in Marcel's love for Albertine and in Earwicker-Tristan's love for Anna-Livia-Isolde.

Once, Greek tragedy and French tragedy of the seventeenth century attained a supreme degree of symbolism. The so-called 'classical' tragedy is the least realistic form of art and the most symbolic. Today, in the novels of Proust and Joyce a realization of the novel is being enacted, at a moment in its history when it justifies itself in a purely symbolic way. The symbolism of tragedy: bare, stripped, severe, and rapid, is replaced by the symbolism of the novel: rich, complex, undulating with the slowness of nightmares and sleep.

In these two literary expressions of the symbol, the tragedy and the novel, there is a single subject: love; and a single character: time. In the tragedy of Sophocles and of Racine, time is rapid, harassing, cruel. It seizes love and destroys it in the space of a few hours. In the novel of Proust and Joyce, time is the slow abiding power which modifies love without destroying it. The modern world has heard new lessons on time and its relativity, but this world of Bergson, Einstein, and Whitehead is not different from the world which the artist has always known and feared. The sonnets of Shakespeare, Proust's novel, and *Finnegans Wake* are all the same world where time plays the principal rôle. If Shakespeare writes in one sonnet:

> *Ruin hath taught me thus to ruminate—*
> *That time will come and take my love away.*
> (*Sonnet* 63.)

and in another sonnet:

> *His beauty shall in these black lines be seen,*
> *And they shall live, and he in them still green.*
> (*Sonnet* 62)

it is to state once more the vigour of experience and the transitory nature of experience. But these two attributes of love: power and decomposition, are creations of time.

Invisible character of the novel, time is also a triptych hero. He creates experience, destroys experience, and

108

makes art possible. Time creates love, creates suffering, and finally effaces suffering. It creates the need of creating art and alone permits the realization of art. Time is the author, director, and actor of this cosmic play we call life.

THE PILOT: SAINT-EXUPERY

i *the poet's subject*

The language of the great novelist always preserves some elements of poetry. Since poetry is the most primitive language of men—language is the ornamentation of thought—it persists even in those novelists who try to abolish it: in a Stendhal, for example, whose *Le Rouge et le Noir* is the least poetic of the great novels; and it rises up in others who, quite naturally, ascribe to it a first place of importance, in a Joyce, for example, whose *Finnegans Wake* is the most poetic of the great novels.

Antoine de Saint-Exupéry is an independent. His language is often poetic, but poetry is not for him a rare or frequent ornament, it is a way of seeing and feeling, an aspect of his sensitivity, a requirement of his nature. The poet in Saint-Exupéry is responsible for the architecture of his novel and for the elaboration of his subject.

The immediate subject of his last novel is the war, the campaign of June 1940, a reconnaissance flight in the north of France, the immense exodus of the people, and their flight toward the south. Behind this first subject of the story, there is another subject more complex and more profound in its meaning: that of Germany against France, of the industrialists against the agriculturists, of the factory against the plough. And these two historical and sociological themes are constantly being converted into the very personal subject of the absurd commission of the air pilot in the midst of a military disaster.

War, historical destiny, and personal experience are the three exterior subjects which Saint-Exupéry translates by means of a single symbol: the airplane. As with a poet, everything is converted in this novelist's book into a symbol, everything is reduced and truncated. Saint-Exupéry's message is not really a message (and we remember that a message is never the important part of a poem): he tells us that the action of war is a spiritual and physical impoverishment. Whereas a book *of* prose always maintains some trace of bombast and attitudes, this new book *in* prose of Saint-Exupéry preserves the invulnerable aspect of a symbol. The plane of Saint-Exupéry is authentically a symbol, like Mallarmé's swan, like Rome in *Bérénice*, like Troy in *Andromaque*. The plane, that is the war, annihilates the work of time, as sin destroys the work of sanctification and creates a new being.

ii *the poet's method*

Pilote de Guerre (*Flight to Arras*) is difficult to classify. In order to translate the life, the mystery, and the multiple meanings of the symbol, a new form of composition is needed for the novel, more specifically suitable to the symbol. In Proust's work, this method is called the stream of consciousness, and in Saint-Exupéry's work, it appears to us to be a variation of this same stream of consciousness. A condensed, violated, and sombre variation.

The poet-novelist's method is that of evoking the entire war in a brutal and lapidary emphasis on a few fragments of a single adventure. The Proustian stream of consciousness is arbitrarily slow, destined to exhaust experiences and sensations. But the art of Saint-Exupéry, created by the collision of violent actions and destructive events, is necessarily concise, destined to reduce the experience and the sensation, desirous of showing a single profile. The secret profundity of these two arts and two methods is incontestable. They show, with many divergences of expression due to historical moments and artistic temperaments, the work of the conscious and the subconscious.

Saint-Exupéry's adventure, congealed in the hard and rapid symbol of the plane, is an adventure that sings; it does not speak and it does not relate. The novelist is a kind of poet because he is the adventurer unashamed of his heart. He never judges. Throughout the work, he remains

110

the man astonished at his own adventure and at the action in which he is engaged. The book, in this respect, becomes a kind of poem composed of a series of images of the present and of the past seen from the airplane. But the poet is always flying over his past and his present: he is the man who releases all the images in order to attain their essence, their source, and their weight.

iii *poetry and catastrophe*

And precisely, the essence which Saint-Exupéry discovers in his images of the sky, of the villages of France, and of the war, is what we are justified in calling catastrophe.

It is not the danger which is central in *Pilote de Guerre*, it is the freedom of danger and the new being whom danger creates. We could justifiably call this new man, in his cruel adventure of heaven and earth, a poet. He traverses night and danger like one more of those poets of night. It is not the same night known so intimately by Nerval and Rimbaud, and neither is it the spiritual night of a Saint John of the Cross. It is the subject of a real sky of stars which weigh heavily over France, the night of a catastrophe extending over the multiple soul of France, a dark night divided by the flight of a plane.

Pilote de Guerre is a poem in prose on the meaning of the lost wager and on the theme of fate. Here we touch on the key of this study: fate is a theme of poetry and not a theme of prose. Poetry is that form of expression in perfect harmony with the most profound and the most hidden principles of human destiny. Prose is always autonomous and liberated from a fatal form. The 'consent to sacrifice' is the principal action of the novel, and this consent revindicates the eternal value of tragedy. As in any great poem, in this novel of Saint-Exupéry, man and God are very close.

Chacun est responsable de tous. Chacun est seul responsable. Chacun est seul responsable de tous . . . Et chacun porte tous les péchés de tous les hommes.

(p. 218)

The catastrophe in France of 1940—we are judging solely

111

from the 'artistic' viewpoint and not from the 'political' viewpoint, which would be quite another story—in the pages of Saint-Exupéry takes on the value of a fatal and static action which bears the impress of a divine will and a universal meaning. A poetic tragedy, according to the precepts of Aristotle, would not be very different.

iv *man in the presence of poetry*

What remains especially charged with poetry and meaning in *Pilote de Guerre* is the symbol of the airplane which, suspended between heaven and earth, bears a man who is thinking. High in the air where he can contemplate the entire catastrophe and feel the agony of his country, this man, like a poet, undergoes a true derangement of his senses.

It is not only June 1940 that he lives through. The country he flies over is larger than France. It is man, and what is purest in man. The language rising up from the heart of this poet who wears an aviator's uniform is a series of lapidary formulas which exceed actuality and forge a new language worthy of a new intensity.

But in the vertiginous adventure of air and space and sun, the goal is suddenly no longer visible, and all that remains is the discipline. All that remains is the poetry when the experience has disappeared. 'Les hommes occupent peu de place dans l'immensité des terres', writes Saint-Exupéry (p. 94). This is a persistent theme in the first part of the book which, farther on, thanks to a Cornelian struggle which grows in the pilot, is transformed into the superhuman meaning of sacrifice, and ends in a meditation on Man and the eventual restoration of Man.

Ma civilisation repose sur le culte de l'Homme au travers des individus . . . Il faut restaurer l'Homme. C'est lui l'essence de ma culture.

(p. 225-6)

This scorn for the useful and the assured recalls another warrior's adventure, that of Jeanne d'Arc, and her struggle against the impossible. This sentiment of human greatness filling the heart of a solitary pilot in the midst of a catastrophe recalls Claudel. Many voices of poets, and of men who have been poets of action are mingled and assimi-

112

lated in this recent voice of our time. A man among us unflinchingly faced the war of our time and knew that it contains the source of man's majesty and of his poetry.

PETROUCHKA

I

Only a straw-stuffed puppet this modern hero! His soul is so tiny that we might almost say he has no soul at all. The flat bright colours of his costumes are the simple basic passions which he has learned by rote and which he typifies under the white grease paint. But his mouth is human in its tortured line and his eyes have at times the light of all of man's prayers and loves. Human in his final convulsions and in his death, he appears only as a caricature of man in his life, an hallucinated clown whose jerkiness and animation depict the comic of passions. The crowd must forget the tragedy of passions. He is the will of the crowd. He is the tawdry projection of the crowd's wilful flight from reality. He is the soul of the crowd when it has no courage and no heroism. Petrouchka is the reminiscence of what was human.

Yet the passion of all past heroes is in the puppet. Petrouchka is in love. Within the sawdust of his awkward body, there is a grain of life which has all the swelling recklessness and all the trembling blindness of Antony and Othello. Love can change a man into a clown and change a clown into a man. Modern literature no longer contemplates the great principle of love in a hero of stature and vigour. As though he were engaged in some laboratory experiment, the creative artist has grafted the principle of love on innocent and helpless replicas of man. Petrouchka's white face against the black walls of his cell shows up clearly. Art is an experiment taking place under a steady flood light. The hero-clown is exhibited, even in his cell and in his solitude, and appears as visible as if he were tied on an operating table. The greatness of his figure has vanished, but the unity of his being is still the same.

113

The divine in him, which is the force of his love, beats against the sawdust walls of his limp body, as he beats against the fictitious cardboard walls of his cell. For there is no greatness, no dignity in his world: the planks he parades on are barely nailed together and the rope which pulls the faded stage curtain seems to break at each night stand. Integrated, pure, tragic, his love for the insipid ballerina dominates the show, melts the greasepaint, releases his spirit in its dance before the ideal.

II

For Plato, a man's love is his search for himself. Without much juggling of terms, this definition can apply to divine love because the self which is sought is that pure part of being, between which being and God there is no obstacle. The clown traffics with the childlike part of himself. When a child desires an object, no amount of reasoning or logic can turn him from his desire. Pierrot, Pinocchio, Petrouchka belong to the race of children who die before their desire is realized. Their fate is a mock tragedy because they have no sense of shame at their plight. Children and clowns never realize that their plight is universal and shared: they are the innocent scapegoats of all the adult and bourgeois spectators who watch half-amused, half-puzzled, in the antics and incarnations of the clown and the child the projection of their own undivulged desires.

And so, love in the puppet, as does love in the prophet, who is still another specimen of the abandoned scapegoat, grows into tragic intensity. Petrouchka's love is the pure symbol of tragedy: rapid, powerful, crushing. His first movements are as futile as the first words of Phèdre. He is already, at the beginning of each performance, in the domain of death. His daily ritual is a flight from a vocation of mimicry and humour into a personal experience of love. There he lives as he had never lived in his showman's trade, and there he dies because of his infidelity to the lesser life.

The contemporary painters realized the clown's tragedy and its depiction of the hero. As all women were in the

114

painted Virgin of the Italian Renaissance, so all men are in the painted clown of modern France. Cézanne, Rouault, Picasso have re-created all the poses of Petrouchka. He lives also in the *Pitre Châtié* of Mallarmé and in the *Orphée* of Cocteau. As in the ballet of Stravinsky and Fokine, Mallarmé's clown makes a hole in his tent and escapes into the world of love where he is struck down with a bolt from heaven. Petrouchka is related to the children of the sun and the race of Phèdre because his love consumes him in its frenzy. If Phèdre has beauty and grace, her desire is depicted as monstrous and grotesque; but the very purity of Petrouchka's desire is deformed by his unnatural body and the exaggerated traits of his countenance.

III

Modern poetry is a world familiar with the spiritual struggle of Petrouchka. In fact, the poet at all times is not unlike the clown. He is the type of man to whom the French word 'chétif' applies. When the poet is not performing as poet, it may well be that he is collapsing or dying somewhere. Mallarmé's faun is comparable to the poet whose experience is never realized, whose experience is never joy. In Hart Crane's *Southern Cross*, the chétif poet wants the 'nameless Woman of the South': his tragedy is that of loving what is impossible and unreal, as Petrouchka's is that of loving what is inferior and unresponsive. The theme of innocency and 'childhood havens' in Ben Belitt's verse is a statement not of love or tragedy, but of a spiritual fervour akin with Petrouchka's fervour and 'faint heart' and abiding oneness. In the recently published *Lincoln Lyrics* of John Malcolm Brinnin, we read a poet struck with the choreographic gauntness and 'graceless strength' of a hero possessing none of the traditional heroic glamour. The space and site of Lincoln's childhood were not epic-marked, but 'acorn-punctuated'. His love was a 'Song of Songs on Illinois'.

The contemporary poet, if he is not Petrouchka himself, sees what is tragic and eternal in Petrouchka. If the poet is not inhabiting the very heart of despair, as Petrouchka and Hart Crane were, he is concerned with the preparation

115

for that despair which he discovers in what Saint Augustine would have called the world of his universal memory.
In a spiritual sense, then, the poet is the clown either because of the total and hysteric absorption of himself in the
object loved, or because of his waiting in the mythic part
of a world which the rest of the world contemplates with
feelings of recognition and amusement and remoteness.

IV

Characters in prose fiction, and some of the most striking in recent times, bear traits of Petrouchka and traces
of his agony. In Flaubert's *Un Cœur Simple*, Félicité is a
counterpart of the puppet. She loved instinctively and
without hope the persons nearest to her until they all died
and she was left with the symbol of frustration: the stuffed
parrot. In this caricature of affection, both hideous and
pathetic, there is the enactment of a clown's strategy.
When Petrouchka is killed by the moor's scimitar, his
body turns out to be only a straw-stuffed figure, and when
Félicité is dying, her ultimate vision of reality is the wide-
spread wings of her parrot mounting heavenward. These
are the heroes who loved what didn't exist and who died
embracing the air.

Such frustration as Félicité's is not reserved solely for
the simple in heart. Aschenbach, in Thomas Mann's
Death in Venice, is the intellectual and artist whose insensate love for the young boy Tadzio, has in it the same mock-
ery and unreality as Petrouchka's love has. A great human
passion lodged in a puppet's body is as tragic as the love
of a mature artist for a young boy to whom he can never
speak. Both are tragic because of their ludicrous unreality.
The puppet, the servant girl, and the artist represent
three levels of existence in which the same tragedy of disproportion occurs. Petrouchka's dance and rhythmic con-
tortions, Félicité's stuffed parrot, which is a kind of relic
of her dead love, and Aschenbach's fever-infested Venice
where he continues to live with Tadzio and death until
his real death comes, are the symbols of what has hap-
pened to each one ; and in each case, it is the symbol of
the irremediable.

116

Even in stories published in 1941, Petrouchka's ghost continues to dictate to his new children the awkward passion of loneliness. *A Memory* in Eudora Welty's book, *A Curtain of Green*, with the delicacy and suggestiveness of a woman's skill in writing, recalls the incident in a young girl's life of a certain morning when she touched her friend's wrist as they passed on the stairs in school. Later, on a beach where she is watching the crude playfulness of a family, she tries to live in her memory of love and in all its pitiful singleness of gesture. The man in the family group pours sand inside his wife's bathing suit between her breasts, and when she stands up, 'the lumps of mashed and folded sand came emptying out . . . as though her breasts themselves had turned to sand'. The image has the same mixture of horror and grotesqueness and comedy as Petrouchka's dance ; and there is the same unreality of the exterior world and the acute prolonged reality of the timid heart.

V

Petrouchka's wake is attended by a vast company. The modern artist has seized upon the dual body of the puppet: the limp straw body stretched out on the market place, and the writhing body of the spirit as it appears over the tent at the end of the ballet. He has recast the dualism of Greek and Judeo-Christian philosophy in the quiescent deathlike Petrouchka and the violent energizing Petrouchka. The ancient problem of appearance and reality is the rapid life story of the puppet. His garb is the clown's and his grease paint is the performer's, but his destiny is suffering and death.

The greatest of all Petrouchkas is James Joyce's Earwicker. Flaccid and melting, half conscious and half asleep, H. C. Earwicker, who is the comic and the tragic of all men, both participates in and watches a long procession of eidolons. Shadows of himself and of all men parade in cinematographic ease through his sleeplessness. Their focal point is love and the nightly seizure of passion. Earwicker lies beside his wife in bed, but a world of time and change is between them. His mind moves out of his body, as Petrouchka's spirit abandoned his punctured straw corpse, and wanders to another bed where his sons sleep. The old man is the young man; the puppet is the lover; the prince is the pumpkin. 'I thought you were all glittering with the noblest of carriage. You're only a pumpkin'.

The first ballet on the programme might easily be *Giselle*: classic, simple, natural, where the hero loves the heroine and she loves him. But *Petrouchka*, which ends the programme, is the modern distortion. The tragedy of *Giselle* is a fairy story and the fairy story of *Petrouchka* is a tragedy.

NARCISSUS

i *myth*

quod cupio mecum est

Narcissus is the myth of the profound present when man looks at himself and questions himself. The fountain, sole element of the setting, is in reality the universe, the choreographic, summarized, and tranquil site of the universe. The dreaming boy, on his first escapade, is praying for the waters of the fountain to sleep. He is praying for a quasi-impossibility: the sleep of all the disorders of the universe, so that he may mirror himself in them, so that he may grant himself the right of seeing himself, of seeing all his contours during the terrible present moment of living. Nature must arrest all change and breathing so that a youth may perceive himself and become his own double!

The child, precociously too tender, is seeking solitude, and, before knowing that the world needs his tenderness and even expects it according to a great principle of love, confides this tenderness to himself in his fixed stare. To become oneself is the law of his happiness. Adam, before the division of himself and the creation of his other form we call 'woman', must have resembled Narcissus and known also a sweet and mirrored self-sufficiency. Adam must have told himself, as Narcissus did, that he would not know any other soul but his own. The destiny of man, since the fleshly divisioning of Adam, has been the search of that part of himself separated and different from himself. And now Narcissus is bent upon opposing this destiny and forgetting it in his horizontal mirror!

Narcissus desires himself. He is no longer the child considering himself with mild curiosity or desirous of seizing the reeds which grow out of the shallow waters near the bank. And he is not yet the man who feels disgust for himself and longs to possess a person other than himself and of a different sex. Narcissus is the adolescent on his knees who has for himself and for the flesh he sees reflected a strange and new desire. He knows for the first time the sensation of death because in his thoughts he is striving in vain to reach himself. While other boys play, battle, and jeer at one another, he discovers his pleasure in the admiration of his own picture, in his love of self. The showing of his body to himself is the sole rite he wishes to perform. Everything in his mind and in his blood rushes toward his lost form which is now rediscovered and which his immobile vision penetrates during these passively lived moments. So pure an androgynist, he sees himself now as man, now as woman. It is vital for him to be duped by this subjective phantom.

And yet Narcissus is modest. By the very slowness with which he contemplates himself and by the long analysis he makes of his features, he proves his scorn for any hasty and rewarding improvisation. His one hesitating smile is really an agreement between two smiles, and from his reflection mounts up to the boy a light which intoxicates him steadily, sweetly. He has no feelings of immodesty which are feelings of facile possession and declamation. Velleities, instincts, sentiments, all disappear save this game invented by him of the image lost and the image seized. Water is the source of his life, but can one embrace an aquatic reflection?

When Narcissus penetrates the intimate meaning of the dormant water, he is actually renewing his own myth and explaining to himself the harsh lesson of his destiny. 'He will live if he doesn't know himself', had predicted at his birth the soothsayer Tiresias. But, as he leans over the water, he is thereby committed to self-knowledge and self-exploration. Death is already touching him, and coveting his flesh. With the first glance which intoxicated him, he entered the full glory of a hero. But the hero, by definition, is a man who has no future. As soon as his deed is accomplished, the life of a hero is a gradual dying. And Narcissus, with his first look, which reveals to him his love for himself, becomes a hero because at that moment he exhausts the triumph over himself. The hero is the man who suddenly stands alone without anything; no principles and no parts of the universe have importance for him any longer. He became, by his deed, the universe for himself, and after his moment of triumph, there is nothing, there will be nothing save the void and the desired annihilation of every day, the wearing out of every minute. The hero and amorous Narcissus equal one another because at the supreme moment, at the moment of sacrifice which is one of self-discovery and self-knowledge, they both desire and will disaster. They extinguish an entire life in one flash, and discover a moment afterwards that what they hold in reality is motionless death.

Narcissus creates his own victory and then takes up exile in it. It is for an instant, but that very instant must subsume the future. What is the action of Narcissus? Of what does his heroism of a youthful exhibitionist consist? Like all heroes, Narcissus wishes to lose what is pure in himself. He seeks what is profoundest in himself in order to extirpate it. The innocency of Narcissus is in danger because for the first time it is tinted with an erotic shade and longs for its own disappearance and death. This is the deep universal present of heroism, the moment known by us all which will be called henceforth the narcissistic moment: conceived is the desire to lose one's unity since this unity, once it has been measured by the senses, exacts its own dispersal! The soul, bending over an abyss of reflections, wills the scandal of a loss, just as military glory wills on various occasions the collective loss of an army or of a nation. Held by his own beauty, unmindful that man should contemplate a beauty other than his own, Narcissus feels himself bound precisely by what will not enrich him. Risk alone increases the stature of man. Narcissus is the hero who runs no risk because he wagers all his being on what is most personal to that being.

ii *figures*

pariterque accendit et ardet

In the evolution of the *libido* Freud indicates three stages, of which the second is primarily essential to this study. The child is interested first in himself and in his own body. When this natural interest is increased by an erotic impulse, the psychologist calls it the narcissistic *libido*. In the normal development of the adolescent this desire is quite quickly transferred to another person. This cycle of three stations has an almost concentric cycle in the customary evolution of the human mind: the child poetizes, the adolescent analyses, the man dogmatizes. Avid for silence, sun, and trees during the first part of his existence, man then devotes an expression of his life to endless discussion and controversy, and finally, after his youth is over, discovers in the traps of bourgeoisism his faith stabilized and silenced in conventions, laws, social equilibrium.

Narcissus, or the modern hero whom I believe we may call Narcissus, stops at the second stage of these erotic-sexual and spiritual cycles. His vision is immaculate and his desire inviolate. What solitary emotion fills him? What strange despotism reigns over his nature which, after very few modifications perhaps, is human nature in its universal state?

The modern world is about ready to recognize in Narcissus one of its most beloved sons, the one of its many captives who has known himself the best and the one who has most profoundly ignored the world in which he lives. This is no ignorance cultivated through some principle, nor is it an absence of sympathy. It is rather an illness comparable to the fever which attached Narcissus to the brink of his fountain. Stendhal's hero, Julien Sorel, is par

121

excellence the nineteenth century. All the diverse types created by the century are in him: René, the pale sensitive lover of nature; Napoleon, the conqueror of battles; Byron, seducer and egoist; Hernani, the fated hero of obscure origin; Perdican, the man who doesn't know whether he is gambling or not with love. *Le Rouge et le Noir* of 1831, which is the most bitter account of Restoration bourgeoisism and pessimism, and of the entire century's, for that matter, is, in spite of its prose texture, made up exclusively of real facts, the most poetic myth of the modern soul. Above all, Julien is Narcissus. He is modern and ancient at the same time, the man of inflexible sweetness. As was the solemn hour of Narcissus which he spent at the edge of the river, Julien's life is composed of hesitations, retractions, inconstancies. He prepares in the desert of each house he lives in, a perverse and secret triumph. A persistent doubt joins him with Narcissus: he knows his love is perishable. He knows each love, each ambition, each dream is perishable. As it was for Narcissus, it is impossible for Julien to distinguish between love, ambition, dream. The absent ones, those who are loved and those who are hated, are only a name. He sees no face save his own.

Behind Narcissus stretches out the world of men, and before him, in the mirror of the pool, the reproduction of his own traits. He is immobilized between the life of action and the life of contemplation. The world fails to attract him and he spends himself in his contemplation of nothingness. Julien likewise is immobilized between the necessity of bending himself to the will of the world and the desire to dominate the world. Thus is explained and reproduced the narcissistic myth of infecund dreams. Sensuous and solitary Narcissus finds his double in wilful and impotent Julien. Narcissus loves without being able to embrace the image of his love; Julien is incapable of loving and tries to attain, through the conquest of his mistresses, to some higher rank. Seated on the rock in the forest, he watches in the flight of the hawk the symbol of his destiny, and becomes, in his imagination, the bird of prey, just as Narcissus, by his steady self-contemplation, makes himself into his own ravisher!

Thirty years after Julien Sorel, Mallarmé's swan (as well as his clown, his faun, his 'terrified Hero' of the sonnet and of *Prose pour des Esseintes*) recapitulates the fate of Narcissus. It is winter. The lake is frozen, but the ice is transparent, and the wings of the swan, uselessly outstretched under the covering of ice, demonstrate the same tragedy of impotent love in their 'flights which haven't flown'. Narcissus incapable of loving, Julien incapable of dominating, and the swan (who is the poet) incapable of creating, are arrested in their existence by the monstrous force of a dream which appears in the form of three kinds of love: love of self, love of the world, love of artistic creation.

The swan, a symbol, white, pure, motionless and dying, is a new reincarnation of Narcissus and Julien, and a new development of the pride which attached them to their destiny of frustration. Narcissus kneeling in his child-like pose of self-adoration, and Julien seated on his rock and contemplating himself in the flight of the hawk, prefigure Mallarmé's swan which, this time, is not held down by his dream or relegated to the limbo of the darkest subconsciousness. He is immobilized, not by himself, but by the hard cold substance of the ice, exiled in the kingdom of frost and snow. The hidden theme of sterility in Narcissus and Julien becomes clear in the white prison of the swan. The inner personal struggle of the hero, so sumptuously composed of eroticism and narcissism, lasted too long. It was surpassed. The world could no longer wait for the hero to recognize the divine and gratuitous beauty of nature, and the simplicity of true love which is self-donation and even self-immolation. Cruelly it closed down over this proud being in increasing its amorous embrace. The gesture which Narcissus could not accomplish and which Julien didn't wish to accomplish, is imposed upon the swan as supreme punishment and verdict of death.

The novels of the twentieth century provide countless examples of narcissistic heroes, but the most astonishingly faithful to the ancient dilemma is Marcel, especially Marcel of *La Prisonnière* who keeps Albertine hidden away from everyone, in the room at the end of the corridor in the Paris house. At Balbec, Albertine belonged to everyone, but in Paris, in the spacious mornings when Marcel awoke, she is a canticle to the glory of the sun, and serves as a mirror for the suffering of Marcel, who looks at himself in her face which he doesn't love but which he needs to possess alone.

All these heroes of Proust: Swann, Charlus, and Marcel are united in their imperious need of seeing and of seeing themselves. They fall in love with the ideal vision of themselves which they discover in someone else. Marcel says, at the beginning of his long narcissistic meditation in which Albertine represents his fountain whose calm and sleep are so grievously indispensable to him, a short sentence which resounds like some explicit condemnation of Narcissus: 'La vérité change tellement pour nous'. (*La Prisonnière*, I, p. 24.) Nothing is stable in the world except oneself. Narcissus does not dare contemplate a force or a beauty different from his own. Marcel will never love Albertine because the principle of love is the absolute (cf. the sonorous first line of Crashaw's poem to Saint Teresa: 'Love, thou art absolute sole Lord'.) and Albertine symbolizes waywardness and temptation.

In Albertine, Marcel sees not only the cause of his suffering, but also the person from whom he has nothing more to learn. The immobility of passion for Narcissus and Marcel is this vision of nothingness: the vision of himself in the case of Narcissus, and the vision of the girl who will give him no joy in the case of Marcel. Their drama is the illusion of happiness, the game of hide-and-seek with oneself regulated by the refusal of running a risk. Marcel contemplates Albertine without feeling any joy, and in the zone of vagueness and solipsism which his contemplation engenders he learns to fear the moment when Albertine will disappear, when he will no longer have even the certainty of his suffering. Narcissus fears the evening, the immense desolation of evening, when he will not be able to see himself in the fountain, as Marcel fears the night into which Albertine will plunge in order to disperse for ever the remorse of the jailer and the too well known beauty of the prisoner.

Narcissus is the myth of life which is really sleep. When all of nature is sleeping, and especially the calm waters of the fountain, Narcissus can see himself purely and possess himself ideally. He captures the passion of tranquillity as another man would seize the most vertiginous moments of passion. In her sleep, Albertine resembles a plant stretched out under the eyes of Marcel, a kind of charming captive in whom all of life is summarized and possessed. In watching Albertine sleep, Marcel feels as complete a joy as that known by Narcissus when he watches himself breathe. And Julien Sorel, the most representative Oedipus of the nineteenth century, falls asleep under the sweet persuasiveness of maternal love. Equal in him are the two forces of dream and action. Everything in society, traditions and the moral code, directs him toward the philosophy of universal nihilism. He lives at the dawn of modern pessimism, after the night of Oedipus and before the noon of his sad partner of the twentieth century, the gigolo, who appears also in the features of the 'voyou' and of the clown.

In his triumph with artifice the clown is a new approximation of Narcissus. He plays tricks on the public as Narcissus plays tricks on love, as Rimbaud played tricks on reason, and as Julien played tricks on God. The clown, as well as the modern plot, illustrates the Baudelairian theory of the lie. He symbolizes the purity of desire and intention. His actions have no moral significance because they are imitated and improvised. In this game, which is for him livelihood and vocation, he has no shame. The soul of the clown has no sense of guilt and no memory of sin. That is why, in a sense, the clown is the modern mystic, the man penetrated with religious sentiment, but always invulnerable. In 'acting' sin, one doesn't commit it. Narcissus simulates sin; he doesn't know it.

All these figures are perhaps the same: Narcissus, Oedipus, Julien, Marcel—or the clown, the voyou, the swan, the gigolo, the angel. Of all beings they are the most humble. They ask nothing from the universe; they don't even ask to live. It is true that their nature is proud and passionate, but they do not inhabit a décor which can easily be replaced. They live under the sign of an impotent desire. They play tricks on their essence and their setting, as the deep-sea diver (so precious to Jean Cocteau) plays tricks on the ocean depths. The deep-sea diver is a man who persists in living despite the entire mass of the ocean capable of crushing him.

Narcissus is the clown of our sentiments. The clown is the gigolo of our actions. The adolescent on his knees before the mirroring of himself (it is the voyou hostile to the eyes of others), and the grease-painted figure playing before a public (it is the voyou hostile to the beating of his own heart), both tragically represent the perversion of purity. The travestied purity of Narcissus and the travestied vice of the voyou are the same experience or the same incompleted voyage to the sensible world. Narcissus who looks at himself without seeing the world, and the clown who looks at the world without seeing himself, are the same hero simultaneously humble and humiliated.

Between Narcissus and the clown lives Hamlet who cannot understand his tragedy. Between the adolescent who hides himself and the man who exhibits himself, lives the mysterious being who is neither adolescent nor man but who is both at the same time. Hamlet desperately seeks solitude in his books and in himself, but the world has taken on for him the image of an immense impalpable circus. Wherever he goes, he is seen; wherever he hides, he is betrayed. The same search for love unites him with Narcissus and with the clown, but he represents a different stage in the search. Between love of self, characterized by Narcissus, and fear of love or even personal negation of love, which we see in the clown, exists Hamlet who struggles equally against the egoism of analysis and the fear of giving himself. Love is the loss of oneself in someone else. Hamlet approaches this, but Narcissus denies the very concept of love, and the clown denies it also, in his own way, by the donation and cosmic dispersal of himself.

126

The sentiment which harms love the most, which deforms it monstrously if it doesn't destroy it integrally, is pity. A sure and subtle poison against love, pity is the vice of the bourgeois and the permanent danger of Narcissus and the clown. The dramatic action of Hamlet is his struggle against pity. Each character in the palace seems capable of awakening in him the sentiment of pity, but Hamlet is conscious of the trap which is the narcissism of his nature. The man who feels pity doesn't love, for pity is something added to our heart which fails to change it fundamentally. Pity is the intermittent virtue, as jealousy is the intermittent malady, of the heart. In the clown's true circus and in Hamlet's impalpable circus the intermittences of pity and jealousy have no place. Pity is the reverse of jealousy, or the mask and disguised principle of jealousy.

The abortive attempts of the modern spirit are lucidly drawn by the artists who have seen in the traits of Narcissus and in the traits which resemble his, a dilemma of an aesthetic and a moral order. But the hero created by the artist is always the artist himself, and the artist is all men of his age, their soul canonized by a tacit agreement between men and their time. All men are mirrored in the artist elected by themselves and in spite of themselves, as the mythical adolescent was mirrored in the clear fountain. History becomes myth, myth becomes history, and the earth today is waiting to see whether man will act or lose himself in the analysis of his imaginary actions.

5: The Grail's Cycle

MAN: RIMBAUD AND HART CRANE

I

THE FORM OF love which is threatened or condemned is the only form treated in literature. The passion of love always maintains its primitive meaning which is that of suffering. There seems to be no variation from this principle in the history of Western literature between the legend of Tristan and the novel of Proust. The art of the story, when contrasted with the art of the poem, resembles the quiet and immobility of a tomb because in a story the banalities and actions of life are constantly cloaking the experience of love. Man can't love without living, except in a poem. And it has to be a certain kind of poem: that heightened burning expression of a metaphor which is love shorn of every lesser feeling and lesser act. So even in *Le Jongleur de Notre Dame* the 'story' is always intervening and threatening the fullness of the juggler's passion. So also in religious poets like Hopkins and Claudel, where their love of God is often experienced in His entire created universe, the art becomes more purely song or contemplation. Between the 'narrative' of love and the 'celebration' of love arising from some projection of God's created beauty, both of which represent a kind of peace or triumphant unity, lies the poem which is closer to being love because it condenses passion into an image. The experience of its composition, of its very construction, is love—and therefore the poem doesn't have to talk 'about' love; and it can't celebrate love because it has found no peace. This is the poetry of Maurice Scève, of Rimbaud, of Hart Crane.

Crane committed suicide in 1932 at the age of 33. His was the artistic temperament thrown against the typical background of American bourgeois living. Ohio, Chicago, New York were the principal settings of his life; the separation of his mother and father was the drama of his early years; his nature—introverted, secretive, capable of revealing itself only to very few friends, sensitive to brilliant colours and beauty—fixed upon the profound problems of existence and happiness, and felt itself thwarted at every effort to achieve harmony and belief. He kept odd jobs in order to earn a living and continue with his writing. In Greenwich Village he became acquainted with the so-called 'little magazines' and with the fashionable literary currents. From a moral viewpoint his life disintegrated in excesses of violence and debauchery. Sexual aberration and drunkenness were the pitfalls in which his spirit wrestled with a kind of desperation. His art became increasingly difficult as his personal life became more and more imbedded in dilemma, more and more twisted by what Crane himself called 'the love of things irreconcilable.' (*For the Marriage of Faustus and Helen*).

He was honest with himself in his violence, honest in his flights to the waterfront dives, honest in the new excessive experiences with which the writing of a poem provided him. There seemed to be no escape from his passionate drama, no saving flight from his desires. In his poetry there is perhaps only one theme capable of being interpreted as that of hope or solution or sublimation. It is the theme of the sea and the sea-spell. The title of Crane's most ambitious poem, *The Bridge*, seems to indicate the symbol of that power in man which can join the finite to the infinite. The sea, which he calls in one of his poems 'this great wink of eternity' (*Voyages II*) points to some other world or to some other worldliness. It is the objectification of the poet's persistent nostalgia for another universe and for a peace which the known universe was unable to give him.

For Crane, as for Melville, under the waves and under the gulfs resound the purest hosannahs. All voices there merge into 'one song'. Over it, the bridge, a kind of 'curveship', lends to God the myth of man. In a sense, then, the bridge is the intercessor and mediator for Hart Crane, the modern mechanistic counterpart of the Virgin who, like Brooklyn Bridge—contemplated by the poet as the statue was contemplated by the juggler in the medieval poem—is 'sleepless' and 'condenses eternity'.

Throughout the various sections of *The Bridge*, images and flashes of phrases constantly recall the cult of the Virgin, her purity, her eternity, her pre-eminent rôle of mediatrix. The secret action of Our Lady on obscure and grotesque lives, the action of her prayers and intercession which is revealed in minute flashes appearing in some of the darkest and most mysterious passages of modern poetry, is a subject of wonderment and speculation. In innumerable examples the Middle Ages taught this power of Mary to consecrate the simplest and even the most deformed work as well as to consecrate a sinful life. As the early Italian painters were entranced with the problem of painting in the same figure the traits of a mother and a virgin, so the modern poets (cf. Hopkins, Claudel, Rilke, Eliot, Crane) have been held and intrigued with the dual nature of Mary: her divinity, the rôle she plays as queen of heaven, and her humanity, the infinite comprehension she has of all the problems of the sons of men.

One entire stanza in the prologue to *The Bridge* could almost come from the litany or some liturgical chant:

> *O harp and altar, of the fury fused,*
> *(How could mere toil align they choiring strings!)*
> *Terrific threshold of the prophet's pledge,*
> *Prayer of pariah, and the lover's cry.*

The first section itself of the poem is called *Ave Maria*, in which Crane presents the character Columbus who symbolizes the beginning of the cultural myth of America. The ocean is designated as an 'amplitude that time explores', but the solitary man Columbus who faces it, equals it with his faith. Columbus invokes the Mother of God for the safe return of his ships:

> *Assure us through thy mantle's ageless blue!*

and his prayer equates the span of water as it disappears

in space and is comprehended by the mind of peace which some men possess.

In *Southern Cross*, another section of *The Bridge*, Crane converts the universal myth of Columbus and America into the personal tragedy of the poet. This is Crane's love song to the woman he is unable to name. The namelessness of his love is God: he calls it thus—and it is stretched across the southern sky as well as across the phosphor wake of his boat. Yet the names of three women flash out from the tragic namelessness of the poet's night:

> *Eve! Magdalene!*
> *or Mary, you?*

This litany is a question, timorous, half-formed, ill-articulated, lost in the noise of the churning waters and the endless expanse of the sky. But the poet, in the formulation of his well-nigh inaudible litany, moves out from a total solitude and namelessness to an apprehension of the namelessness of Mary which is on another level. It is perhaps more on this page than on others that Crane's human suffering attains a mystical justification.

Hart Crane is the American poet of the sea, as well as the poet of steel and soil. He lacked the heritage of an intellectual or religious system of thought, which in the case of major poets such as Dante, Milton, Eliot, Yeats, serves as sustenance or background for their personal and their poetic experience. Crane was more alone. The final despair which overcame him was the logical result of his solitude, his oneness, his isolation. Drunkenness was his principal release from solitude. He exemplified the thought of William James that 'drunkenness expands, unites, and says Yes'. His art, as contrasted with that of his sober contemporary, Mr T. S. Eliot, is the art of a drunken spirit: the physical words totter and capitulate before strange places, whereas their images and intuitions rise up from that expanded other realm of drunkenness.

The intoxicated uniqueness of Crane, and his estrangement from any recognizable system of thought or belief, cause him to resemble the performer set off from the public which considers him without very much understanding or sympathy. The clown, the juggler, and the poet are

131

all fused in Hart Crane. Like the twelfth century juggler of Our Lady, Crane sought a public worthy of consecrating his life and his work. The juggler's dance and Crane's verses are the same testimonial to what was best, humanly speaking, in both men.

Crane begins his poem *The Visible the Untrue* with the words:

> *Yes, I being*
> *the terrible puppet of my dreams, shall*
> *lavish this on you—.*

After *Southern Cross*, with its religious overtones and its invocation of Mary, this poem is the other personal statement of the poet who now sees himself as the puppet or clown. The expanse of ocean in *Southern Cross* pointed toward a possible paradise and a possible knowledge of Mary's grace. But *The Visible the Untrue* is a poem of purely human kindness and unkindness. The clown has had to learn how to banish hope and exist solely in his performance.

> *I'm wearing badges*
> *that cancel all your kindness.*

Whereas the medieval juggler's art was performed in a knowledge of faith, hope, and love, the modern poet's art is composed in the knowledge only of love.

There is a further example of the poet's identification of himself with the buffoon in the poem *Chaplinesque*, written by Crane in 1921 after he had attended a performance of Charlie Chaplin's current film of that year, *The Kid*. Crane and Chaplin are united in being the timid modern hero, the 'chétif', who has to content himself with 'random consolations'. But in their timidity and severed lives they know a love for the world which is peculiarly theirs. Crane's love for the city and his stimulation derived from the crowds in the city are equal in their intensity to Chaplin's deep understanding of the common man and his power of tragi-comedy over the vast masses of people who attend the cinema. Crane's love of humanity is reminiscent of Walt Whitman's, and the touching symbol he uses in *Chaplinesque* of the kitten which he has heard in the wilderness evokes a strong connotation of the Gospel

132

story of John the Baptist. The man who loved the sea is the same as the poet-puppet and Our Lady's acrobat in their identical quest for love, immortality, and paradise.

The same process of identification becomes more complex, more deeply religious, and more cosmological in Crane's poem, *Lachrymae Christi*. Here, in the final lines, three figures seem to be invoked and equalized: Dionysus, Christ, and the modern artist. The image is that of the cross, and the crucified smile of all three faces is apostrophized by Crane as the 'target smile'. Three ages and three tragedies are merged into one. Dionysus, the Nazarene, and the buffoon are the same target for the same world's cruelty. The earth around them, like a grail, seems to exist for the principle of their sacrifice.

II

The 'irreconcilable' which the artist meets on various sociological and psychological levels is always at the core of his major experience, and explicitly so in Crane, and also in Rimbaud with whose poetry Crane felt strong affiliation although he was unable to read it easily in the original. Their experience and temperament were so similar that there was little need for Crane of literal translation of Rimbaud's texts. Both Rimbaud and Crane were unable to recognize or feel themselves a part of the bourgeois platitudinous world into which they were born. They both sought a world that could be recognized, that existed somewhere, that was 'dimensional'. But they knew that the world would become dimensional and explicable only when love existed in harmony with the universe. The love of the artist for his work seems to exist in the modern world when he has a sense of the irreconcilable in the other domains of love: the love of man for woman, or the love of man for God. Hence, the artist completes on one level a reconciliation between himself and the world which was impossible for him on another level.

Between life and art there will always extend an abyss of physical and psychic anguish. 'I meet you therefore in that eventual flame', says Faustus to Helen in Crane's poem, and thereby states the meeting between the poet and beauty, a meeting wholly improbable without the flame of experience. And it is precisely within that flame of experience where glows the paradox of the irreconcilable. 'L'air de l'enfer ne souffre pas les hymnes', said Rimbaud. Experience is the punishment for Crane and Rimbaud, and in that room of fire there is no peace and no possible canticle celebration of love.

The first part of this drama of the irreconcilable is the specific rôle of man which his nature imposes upon the artist. Rimbaud and Crane were riveted to homosexuality in much the same way that a convict is riveted to his chain. They could look at the river and the sea and discover there a kind of poetic freedom, but only after the contemplation of their own hearts had drugged them with bitterness and frustration. There is a striking parallel in the desire of both poets to live with primitive peoples, in Rimbaud's return to the negroes of Africa, in Crane's visits to sailors' dives and Mexico. The need to cohabit with those of a primitive nature or at least of a different nature from one's own unquestionably has a strong sexual motivation. To become god of the savages for Rimbaud would equate the attainment to sexual freedom and satisfaction. If one can't copulate with a woman of one's own society, one can with a woman of another race, of another skin and creed. Rimbaud and Crane never emerged from the drama of puberty when there is so strong a temptation to love in contradiction to the laws of nature. The sexual experience of puberty is harassing and insoluble because it is an effort to know one's own sex without going beyond it. This is the dilemma of the homosexual who, of the sex act, knows only its aspect of death and never its meaning of birth. Copulation, or even the desire for copulation, without the death and the birth together is the darkest and most insoluble experience of man. On the one hand, Arthur Rimbaud, in the prophetic trances of his late adolescence saw himself as a god among the primitive negroes, and was in reality the slave to his own nature and an outcast from the bourgeois society of Charleville and Paris. And on the other hand, Hart Crane, in the poems he wrote between the ages of twenty and thirty, saw himself as the artist in the midst of the normal bourgeois of Chicago and New York, and was in reality the clown among the sailors and the tough boys of the waterfront bars. But both, in their art attain a purity, a Platonic purity, unknown to the ordinary artist. Crane calls it, in his most beautiful poem (*Voyages* III):

> *The silken skilled transmemberment of song*

and we recognize the same purifying principle by which, in art, experience is not hidden but intensified and passes beyond morality, as in the sonnets of Shakespeare and in the paintings of Michelangelo.

The drama of the irreconcilables in the heart of man is never separated from the drama of the irreconcilables in the universe of man. In the poetry of Rimbaud and Crane the image of a body of water, whether it be the sea or the river, is the persistent symbol of the universe. It is the cruellest of symbols, the mightiest, and the most inhuman, the element of nature man is least able to embrace or comprehend. The imaginative experience of Rimbaud is his flight down the river into the fullness of the ocean, the bitterness he feels there in the total expanse and depth of colour, and his subsequent return, not to the river but to the caricature of water fertility in the muddy pool of the city street. The combined spiritual and geographical flight he describes in both *Bateau Ivre* and *Une Saison en Enfer* is a restatement of the romantic heresy of attempted life in unreality, and also a denial of the experience's validity. The actual life story of Rimbaud in his escape from the ancient parapets of Europe to the exotic countries of Africa and Asia and his ultimate return to the hospital in Marseille precisely parallels the voyages in his literary testament. And likewise, the imaginative experience of Hart Crane, as related in *Atlantis*, the culminating section of *The Bridge*, where the sea subsumes all voices and all times, where we read the sea's drama which is formed by the extinguishing of other elements, parallels the literal experience of his suicide. Whereas Rimbaud makes a rapid exploration of the sea's myth and returns from it to the bare reality of land, Crane never exhausts its cruelty and finally espouses it when he hurls himself in death into its very centre. The myth of Europe tortures Rimbaud and he tries to get beyond it into pre-Christian primal times. But this myth exists and Rimbaud's tragedy is pure and classic, whereas the myth of America which Crane tries to comprehend is not yet fully created, and his tragedy is caricatured and truncated. Europe was too old for Rimbaud, and America was too young for Crane, as the homosexual is always too old as a boy and too young as a man.

Behind Rimbaud and Crane, and fully known to both of them because he possesses their temperament and prefigures their art, stands Charles Baudelaire. He is their ancestor but endowed with a knowledge of women, possessing a love and hate of women, and possessing also a knowledge of good and evil. In the commingling of the love and tenderness Baudelaire felt for his mother, he learned about the heart of woman, about love and despair, about love and hate, about good and evil; but Rimbaud, as is very often the case with a certain kind of homosexual, hated his mother even as a young boy. Not only is woman absent from the work of Rimbaud, but a real misogyny or hate of woman resounds through many of his poems. If Baudelaire knew the difference between good and evil, Rimbaud doubted this difference and was tormented with not knowing it. Crane was less tormented than Rimbaud, but he felt and acknowledged a lack of terror which helped to create many of the greatest pages in *Une Saison en Enfer*.

The rôle of woman in a poet's work is closely associated with his feeling about the problem of good and evil. The poet's rite is his transformation of the universe into his own poetic universe. He counterfeits the essential gesture of the priest, and poetry, which is the changed substance, remains inviolate. The muse of poets is perhaps simultaneously Eve and Our Lady. Neither saint nor profane, the muse resembles all women and is no one of them. With Hopkins and Péguy she is the Virgin, with Baudelaire she is the infinity of carnal desire, with Rimbaud and Crane she is mystery—neither sacred nor profane—more explicitly than ever the muse, for this name was invented to disguise mystery and hide the imperishable impulse of man toward woman.

Rimbaud and Crane are two of those essentially tragic artists who, rather than forming a part of the large cycle of their period, form complete cycles in themselves. Rimbaud went through the three phases of revolutionary, visionary, and messiah, which easily equate the phase of human love (when the boy hated his mother and loved the workmen as they returned home in the evening: cf. *Poètes de sept ans*), the phase of philosophical love (when the boy became poet in the mysterious alchemy of words: cf. *Sonnet des voyelles*), and finally the phase of divine love (when the poet sought more than the creation of poetry in his ultimate prophetic writings: cf. *Une Saison en Enfer*). These phases are summarized and reversed in a sentence of *Adieu*, the final section of the *Saison:* 'J'ai créé toutes les fêtes, tous les triomphes, tous les drames.' The cycle of Crane is described in *Three Songs* of *The Bridge*. In the first, the poet, incapable of loving woman, seeks the love of God; in the second, he states the pure void of lust; in the third, he transcends lust in his desire for purity and Platonic love. Hence, in Crane, these three phases of religious tragedy, sexual experience, and song reproduce in their own way the major cycle of divine, human, and philosophic love. But in all the stages of Rimbaud and Crane, in Rimbaud's revolutionary-visionary-messianic cycle, and in Crane's religious-sexual-canticle cycle, the poet remains the puppet tormented by the absence of love he feels within him and by his straw-stuffed body which, on every level of experience, can only depict the burlesque of his desire.

III

The mighty symbol of water surrounds and submerges especially those heroes who know that love is condemned and who seek an unknown holiness: Icarus, Prometheus, Rimbaud, Crane. Their sea is comparable to the chapel for Our Lady's juggler, and his swaying body resembles the ceaseless motion of the waves. The juggler has discovered in the statue the necessary immobility which provides a reason for his curious antics and his restlessness. The necessary bridge immobilized across the water is the religious statue for Crane. But Rimbaud's boat is never moored and at the end of its drunkenness its keel collapses and it sinks into the depths. But Rimbaud knew of the fixed lighthouses of Baudelaire and the imprisoned albatross and the limitless hope of innocency. The Virgin is innocency and steadfastness for the juggler, as the bridge and 'the seal's wide spindrift gaze toward Paradise' are the same symbol for Crane.

Le Jongleur de Notre Dame is a composed and contrived story to illustrate the spiritualization and sanctification of a grotesque act. The poetry of Hart Crane has no similar theme or coherence. Man's double adventure with evil and grace is not narrated in both juggler and poet, but each, separately, exemplifies one half of the dual adventure. The juggler, unsuspecting during the final dance before the Virgin's statue, was already the man so solicited by grace that his movements and capers were propelling him into another world. Hart Crane, with an intimate knowledge of his disintegration during the final months of his life in Mexico, was already the man so solicited by evil that his plunge into the ocean from the boat on its way back to New York was not only a tragic culmination to his life but a purifying one as well. The clown's final dance joined him to eternity because of its spiritual intention. Crane's suicide joined him to the major symbol of his poetry—the sea—in which he had sought as an artist a release and a sanctification, in which he ultimately found as a man an end of suffering and an escape from himself.

The final moments for both the juggler and Hart Crane were therefore moments of participation and identification: the clown participated in a dance made sacred by its identification with worship ; Crane participated in the ocean depths and thereby identified himself with the purest, the most expansive, and the most paradisaic principle of his art.

138

The tragic core of *Nightwood* drains the novel of accessories and rhetoric. The work, almost in spite of itself, is
fused into one piece. In this admirable writing, Miss Djuna
Barnes has obeyed the sins of her characters as if they,
only, represented the laws of her novel. The characters
themselves forced *Nightwood* to be what it should be: the
pure depiction of tragedy, as the very nature itself of
Phèdre forced Racine to write a pure tragedy.

A character in tragedy exists alone in the strong floodlight which the artist is able to throw upon him. Oedipus,
Othello, Hermione stand alone not only in the floodlight
of the stage but also in the floodlight of their language
which, rising up from their own subconscious and conscious selves, casts them into such relief that the world of
spectators in the pit before them and the world of other
characters around them on the stage, can have no thought
of touching them. Without the theatric floodlight, *Nightwood* succeeds in presenting characters of deep solitude
illumined by the very darkness of their world. The tragedy
is so authentic and sustained in this novel that it takes on
the excessive luminosity of a circus where, in the story itself, one of the important meetings takes place.

A character becomes tragic because of his strangeness
and his greatness (which may be a quality of monstrous-
ness). He is tragic first because of what he is, secondly because of where he is, and thirdly because of what he tries
to do. There are two sets of tragic characters in *Nightwood*. The first set, Felix and Robin, are dramatic and
move about; the second set, Nora and Matthew, are static
and immobilized in their spiritual paralysis.

Felix is tragic because he is a Jew in Europe of the twentieth century during the very years 'entre les deux guerres'
when the greatest massacre of Jews was being prepared and scientifically planned. What he wants most of
all is a son, and then a title for his son which will give the
boy that strange worldly security which the modern Jew
at times seems to equate with the re-establishment of God

within himself. Robin is tragic because she is the girl who is really a boy. She wanders through the night because to see herself in the day would be to see what the world sees. Night is the confusion of day, as Robin is the confusion of sex. Night is that space of time suspended between two days of light and incapable of vision; as Robin is one of those human beings, suspended between men and women, incapable of asking for, or receiving, mercy. Light is mercy. To see oneself is to be saved.

Felix and Robin marry: Felix, in order to justify himself; Robin, in order to deceive herself. Their son, Guido, is the weakling of impoverished health and unattractiveness, in whose heart burns the fire of purity and faith which had been diverted in Felix's estranged Judaism and Robin's estranged sex. Robin enters the Catholic Church but is unable to ask for mercy. Felix approaches the Catholic Church as a centre of security and social affirmation. It is only the boy Guido, a monster in the eyes of the world, who experiences the pure fire of love, and who, in the presence of his father's drunkenness in the night café, presses a holy medallion against his flesh. The strange lives of Felix and Robin find a justification, unknown to them, in their offspring Guido, who, like the child of fairy stories and mythical patterns, seems to have been conceived supernaturally. Felix loses himself in drunkenness in order to cease looking for the handsome son who will bridge the gap between his race and the aristocracy of Europe. Robin loses herself in promiscuity, in the drunkenness of her senses in order to forget her mistaken motherhood and to escape a love which has no roots in her faith. Guido loses himself in purity vouchsafed to those of imperfect bodies, in the pure intoxication of a child's love for God, which might well redeem the weaknesses of his parents.

In the second set of *Nightwood* characters, Nora and Matthew, less childlike and mobile than their counterparts Felix and Robin, depict a deeper and more tragic state in the permanency of their suffering. Nora is eternally waiting in her house. Matthew is eternally waiting in the *Café de la Mairie du V^{ie}* . The doctor replaces the

140

baron: both Matthew and Felix have questionable titular authenticity. The impermissible blood of the Jew Felix becomes the impermissible desire of the homosexual Matthew. But there is a marked difference in the degree of their suffering and the extent of their tragedy: Matthew is solely responsible for his state but Felix is the pathetic victim without the greatness of personal responsibility. His crime was that of having been born into a persecuted race, and to remedy this he turns Christian. But Matthew was born a Catholic and never ceases believing in Catholicism, although he, like Robin, is unable to ask for mercy from the Church.

Nora, like Phèdre, seeks for permanence in the very character who is the most unsuited to permanence. Love, which is the principle of stability, and which always tries to create within itself a design for the future and a form of permanency, is attracted toward the beauty of youth, toward the impermanent and transitory heart, as if its very principle were its death and dissolution. Throughout *Nightwood* Robin is as fixed and permanent in the heart of Nora as she is impermanent and passing in the night. The heart (who is Nora) is the quiet fixed repository of love where the one loved never fully enters, and the night (who is Robin) is the formless boundless risk where love is never met with except in the form of a ghost or a mask.

Nora's love is a religious worship, but there is no safety in the object of her faith. Her love traverses the novel as a tree traverses the night, but the main action of the story takes place outside of her. The main action is perhaps the carriage ride of Jenny (Chapter 4), who is the 'squatter', the summarized infidelity of Robin, the inferior heart, the one who is not the permanent tree growing in the night. Again like Phèdre, Nora is unable to participate in any action, because, from the beginning, her heart reaches its extreme limits and knows itself, its night and its day, its life and its death, its desire and its accomplishment. A carriage drive through the Bois is an adventure of risk and chance, a grouping together of all the lesser hearts who refuse to know themselves. Nora has only to wait, in the night of her house, as Phèdre has only to wait, in the full light of the sun.

In a sense, it would seem that Matthew is the real protagonist, the central hero of the book. But this hypothesis appears to us now radically false. Nora is the one who questions and who contains the innocent greatness of the hero. As we watch Nora come out of the night, in which she has been waiting, in order to question Matthew, who knows everything about the human soul, even the key to its salvation, and then return back into her night, her questions still unanswered, we know that she is the hero. Matthew answered her questions fully and brilliantly. His words are the most profound in the book. They are the thought of the book, the rich texture necessary to throw into relief Nora's innocency. Her suffering is pure, untried, unrelieved. She is the hero because she has nothing beyond her feelings, no space beyond her which she can fill up with words invented to explicate or twist her feelings. Matthew abdicates his rôle of hero in one of his major statements: 'None of us suffers as much as we should, or loves as much as we say'. (p. 173). Matthew knows evil through truth. Nora knows evil, or rather the suffering of evil, and has forgotten truth.

Matthew therefore, like Charlus in Proust's novel, is the most important character, but he is not the hero. The hero's heart must have wonderment in order to provide the necessary depths for suffering and lack of knowledge. On the heroic heart everything must react virginally. And for it, everything signifies one thing, one love subsuming the universe, attracting unto itself all moving particles like some magnet of the material world or some god of the spirit. The hero is never drunk or monotonously sinful. Matthew's drunkenness and Charlus' incessant and varied sexual experiences preclude in their nature any real tragic heroism or stature. Any repetitive carnal indulgence transforms the possible hero into the ordinary man as surely as any frequent and casual intercourse with the world transforms the possible artist into the bourgeois citizen. The hero is still the one who is lost in wonderment and for whom one act or one person involves and surpasses the universe. Nora is the hero of *Nightwood* because her love is that of a hero, incapable of realizing itself, frustrated by its very virginity and totality, lost by its oneness which is unable to comprehend the apartness of Robin and the nightly divisionings of her passion.

The final scene in the novel, the briefest and most dramatic, is the only one where the action of the characters and their setting are perfectly fused, where, as in some classical fugue, the elements answer one another in even, controlled tones. (Elsewhere, the speech of the characters intercepts their action and effaces the lines of the rooms, the cafés, the streets.) But in this ultimate scene, in America, the chapel takes on a reality of its own, and commands an equal part in the swift violent action which terminates the work.

The imbedded and only half-concealed theme of bestiality and demonic possession in *Nightwood* rises clearly, for the first time, in these last five pages. The setting for its revelation is a chapel lit by two candles on an altar before a Virgin. A Catholic chapel lost in a rural district of Protestant New England is the final scene of this novel about Americans who had sought in Paris the distractions of love as well as the strange sequence of love. Here meet, in a wildly incongruous setting, the two forces which have waged the tragedy: on the one hand, the supernatural force of evil, expelled from Nora's dog and invested in the body of Robin; and on the other hand, the supernatural force of good drawing Robin to the altar before which literally she performs the antics of evil .

The novel ends with a dance of eroticism and death. Robin performs before the altar of Our Lady the rôle .of the character she has become through her knowledge of sin, in much the same way that the juggler of Notre Dame, in the twelfth century French poem, performs as homage of adoration his dances and acrobatics. Like the *jongleur* in the medieval French chapel, Robin stands in her boy's trousers, in the middle of the secluded New England chapel, ready to perform in her mimicry of a dog and in her barking of a dog, the one kind of confession she is able to make. Her confessor is a statue of the Mother of

God; her penance is the loss of human characteristics. The juggler offers the portrayal of his clown's tricks and Robin offers the portrayal of her sin, but one is adoration and the other is confession.

Nora, who watches from the chapel door this final scene of demonic possession, still remains the hero and still remains immobile. She collapses on the edge of the scene of horror she is witnessing, but her body, inert against the wood, is one more offering which Robin, unconsciously perhaps, is making to the Virgin, one other offering added to the flowers and the toys she placed on the altar itself before commencing her dance of confession. To watch Robin as the dancing boy before the statue of the Madonna, and to watch the dog exorcized and whining like some impotent scapegoat relieved of his guilt, would require from Nora the fortitude of a saint. The human drama unfolding in the dimly lit chapel is her own and she succumbs before it as the hero succumbs to the defect of his character when tragedy rises up about him in order to stifle in a flash all the human greatness his life has composed.

When the hero is woman, as in *Nightwood* and *Phèdre*, he resembles the earth and the inertness of matter from which the hero, when he is man, as in *Ulysses* and *Hamlet*, is eternally seeking to tear himself. It is only when Nora loses consciousness that Robin is able to play implicitly the rôle of man and disengage herself from the earth's unmovableness. Her dance is not only the objectification of her sins, but is also the cutting loose from the principle of love which had held her down. It is the symbol of Nora's defeat, the undoing of that steady prolonged awareness of love which traverses all the scenes in the novel like some necessary umbilical cord.

The great tragic scenes in literature have some affinity, either vague or precise, with the circus, and their characters often bear a strong resemblance with the clown. Works as different from one another as Dante's *Inferno*, *Hamlet*, *Le Misanthrope*, Proust's novel, and *Finnegans Wake*, which are among the greatest of the creatively tragic books in literature, all contain scenes of a circus quality where the characters are so knowingly and piteously portrayed that, in their estrangement from the ordinary heart and ordinary existence, they appear as freaks. A certain kind of great literary work is like a 'side show' where human weakness and even human greatness are illumined and demonstrated in comic distortion and travesty. *Nightwood* has this quality: the jests and maledictions of Matthew are projected through the art of his melancholy wit; Robin stalks the night like an 'uninhabited angel'; Felix translates a Jew's undoing as God's. The characters of *Nightwood* form a closely-knit universe, but, outside of Nora, there is no pure sorrow in the work, only confusions. The confusions of the several ring circus are necessary to permit us to bear the pure tragedy of Nora, as the confusions of ordinary living allow us to bear the pure tragedy of our soul.

*   *   *

The novel of Djuna Barnes is apart from most literary works in its performed quality. Its art reminds us of the choreographic art of Miss Martha Graham and the vocal art of Mme Povla Frijsh. These three women, each in her own field exemplary of a rare power of artistic projection, possess a similar kind of sensitivity which, through being profoundly personal, becomes in art, that is, in its creation and performance, universalized. Graham's dance on Emily Dickinson's life, *A Letter to the World*, Frijsh's singing of Debussy's *Le Balcon* (Baudelaire) or Poulenc's *Voyage à Paris*, and Djuna Barnes' writing in *Nightwood* are the highest achievements of contemporary women artists, both creative and performing. They succeed in putting outside of themselves something that was very centrally of themselves. These works participate in consecration and sublimation. They are 'histrionic' in a remarkably pure sense that few men are able to achieve, perhaps no male artists of our age, with the possible exceptions of Henry Miller, André Gide in a few of his volumes, and Proust and Joyce in all of their books.

We are able to read certain passages in *Nightwood*, of such original and resilient texture, that they form themselves outside of the pages and outside of us, as we have heard certain songs sung by Povla Frijsh take on in the air before her a new body, carved by the deep and almost liturgical concentration of the artist, and suspended for a fraction of time, in a world of their own. These women artists, Barnes, Frijsh, and Graham, to whom we might add the extraordinary accomplishments of Nazimova in pure acting and of Wanda Landowska in the playing of the harpsichord, perform more with their total fervour than a man, because of his nature and intermittent fervour, could ever perform. Their art is a dedication and a kind of priestcraft, comparable to the juggler's dance, unashamedly and almost desperately performed, as though at the moment of their ritual they became a primitive principle or source, in objectifying and transcending their state of human being.

THE CHILD: ELIOT AND TCHELITCHEW

i *four quartets'*

Since the time of the medieval poems on the Holy Grail legend and since the *Divine Comedy*, the major works of literature have dealt more exclusively with the tragedy of love than with the quest for love. But in his *Four Quartets*, Mr Eliot has composed a poem unlike the literary work of his contemporary peers, in that his unnamed hero (who is, of course, on one level of interpretation the poet himself) is the quester, a modern Parsifal traversing the dangers and the dryness of the world in his search for the grail castle. In accordance with the modern tradition, the hero of *Four Quartets* is a diminished personality comparable to the clown of the painters and Prufrock of Eliot's earlier poem. Like Emily Dickinson, he is saying throughout all the pages:

I'm nobody! Who are you?

and like Rilke in *Das Lied der Waise:*

Ich bin niemand und werde auch niemand sein.

He is the undeveloped and the undifferentiated one, the clown who performs best before a public of children, as

146

uncharacterized and as unportrayed as the hero in *Une Saison en Enfer*.

Burnt Norton, first of the *Quartets*, is the poem of the rose garden. It is the first world of the children, not the world we actually lived in, but the mythic world constructed by our child's imagination, the perfect rose garden of the fairy stories and the great legends of the children of men. *Burnt Norton* evokes the gardens of the medieval romances as well as 'tous les paysages possibles' of Rimbaud. The child's moment is the exhausting of time and age: the moment when one is all characters, all sexes, all ages—the prodigiously unreal moment when we bear most of reality. Everything is unseen and unheard in childhood. And yet it is the moment when we see and hear the most, when we see the blooms of the rose garden we never entered and hear the birds that sing there.

The second quartet, *East Coker*, is the poem of growing old. It represents therefore an opposing movement to *Burnt Norton* which described the static moment of childhood in which we grew wondrously. *East Coker* is the literal growth and decay, the cycle of the family and of human ugliness. After the first quartet with its strong theme relating the triumph of imagination, the second quartet resounds with the eternally imminent danger of emotion. After leaving the world's garden of our childhood, we enter the earth's hospital of our maturity.

The last two quartets are religious interpretations of the first two: *The Dry Salvages*, the third quartet, interprets *East Coker*, the second, and *Little Gidding*, the fourth poem, interprets *Burnt Norton*, the first. The real world and its principle of growth and change are first interpreted in *The Dry Salvages*, by the image of the sea, symbol of timelessness, and the symbol of the bone on the beach, image of man's fate in time. The strange drama of human flesh becomes comprehensible to Eliot only in terms of the 'calamitous annunciation' of man's fall and that other Annunciation of the Redeemer's birth. The destructive element of time and the wasting of human flesh are offset by the prayer of the Lady on the promontory and the doctrine of the Incarnation. The timeless explains the timed, as the spirit explains the body, as the sea explains the river, as the Annunciation explains the Incarnation.

In the final quartet, *Little Gidding*, the springtime of *Burnt Norton* has become midwinter spring and the rose garden has become a secluded chapel. The roseate imagined world of the child has become England in the early 1940's darkened by the menaces and the knowledge of war. To the doctrines of the Annunciation and the Incarnation succeeds the doctrine on Love: the descent of the Holy Spirit in the form of Pentecostal fires. The language of the dead is superior to the language of the living. It is tongued with fire and communicates to the timed from the timeless. From the Heraclitean sentences on the death of air and earth, and of water and fire, to the allusions concerning air warden patrols in England—from the Pentecostal fire to the flickering tongues of the Messerschmitts, a tremendous span in time is effaced.

The evolution of Mr Eliot's work parallels the cycle of *The Divine Comedy*. *The Waste Land*, with its persistent theme of dryness and sterility, its interrupted dramatic episodes on frustration, its nightmarish and static quality, is the *Inferno* where the modern world is seized by its own guilt and transfixed by its own conscience. In this first major poem of Eliot, time is held within itself as though it could never be redeemed. The movements in it, as in Dante's *Inferno*, are not progressive, they are endless repetitions and their visions are the dry landscapes already seen. *Ash Wednesday* marks the transition from the first period of Eliot's poetry to the most recent volume, as *Purgatory* involves on the one hand the total understanding and memory of sin, and on the other hand, the promise that with sin's acknowledgment and repentance the end of its realm will be reached. *Four Quartets* are not in any literal sense a poem on *Paradise*, but they bring the spirit of man, the modern man who has made the absolute turning of *Ash Wednesday*, to the very frontier of the third realm where the suffering of indifference and ignorance (*The Waste Land*) and the suffering of spiritual knowledge (*Ash Wednesday*) are converted into the suffering of Love (*Little Gidding*).

The rose bush and the yew tree are constantly recurring symbols in Mr Eliot's work, used to designate time and eternity. The leaves of the shrubbery, mentioned in the opening lines of *Four Quartets*, and the apple tree growing in the same garden, referred to in the final lines of the work, form a major theme in the elaborate musical construction. The tree moves in its leaves as the entire sky seems to move in the drift of its stars, but one is the movement of time, exhausting itself and recommencing, and the other is the movement of eternity, absolute in itself, conquered and conquering. As in Mallarmé's remarkable sonnet, *M'introduire dans ton histoire* (drawn upon heavily by Mr Eliot in *Burnt Norton*, part II, especially in the opening line: 'Garlic and sapphires in the mud' which recasts 'Tonnerre et rubis aux moyeux'), there is a strong relation in *Four Quartets* between the human timed drama taking place on the earth, 'nu gazon de territoire', and the timelessly omnipresent Divine Love flashed across the heavens like the permanent sun.

Perhaps more than a relation between the cycle of human life: its birth, fulfilment, and death—and the never exhausted, never changing energy of Divine Love, there exists an intersecting or a collision when, on one level, the bread becomes the Real Presence, and on another level, when man, while remaining held in time, transcends it in his sudden apprehension of Love, and when, on still another level, God or His spirit of timelessness and excessive Love, enters a body He created for His own reception. This drama of collision which permits man to comprehend, bear, and transcend the great principle of flux in which he lives, is the drama of *Four Quartets*. The hero is the quester, the searcher for that moment in time which is timeless and always, the visionary of all the possible landscapes, the prototype of Parsifal whose vision of the grail is the prepared and explicit moment of his salvation. And like Parsifal, the quester in *Four Quartets* relies upon the children in the tree for direction.

The purity of the children's voices can be apprehended

only by the pure in heart. Verlaine, in his sonnet on *Parsifal*, breaks off the narration of the grail ceremonial at the precise moment of elevation, as in the mass, and with his fourteenth line: 'Et ô ces voix d'enfants chantant dans la coupole' (used in *The Waste Land*) translates the moment of religious ecstasy by evoking the purity of boys' voices. In the Holy Grail legend, Parsifal is guided to the grail castle by the voices of children in the tree (as Siegfried followed the voice of a bird), and in these new poems of T. S. Eliot, the poet is guided by the voices of children and birds hidden in the shrubbery and rose bushes of a child's garden (*Burnt Norton*) to the secluded chapel of his mature faith (*Little Gidding*).

The symbol of the tree is all important, whether it be the rose, testifying to carnal love in the child's first sexual experience and hence to the principle of change and decay, or whether it be the yew tree, which, like the grail castle and the Anglican shrine of *Little Gidding*, testifies to the permanency of Divine Love. In the medieval tradition the tree can easily be explained on the four levels of interpretation: first, as the literal tree in the setting of Eliot's rose garden; secondly, as the allegorical tree of the Crucifixion from the top of which the Voice speaks and directs; thirdly, as the tropological tree whose life cycle is the moral divisioning of time; and fourthly, as the anagogical tree when, suddenly, at the end of the final poem, it is called the apple tree and alludes, as does the spitting out of the apple seed in *Ash Wednesday*, to the spiritual drama of man's fall and redemption. As the tree in the first garden was the gauge or barometer of man's obedience and love, so the tree in Eliot's poems is the symbol of time and eternity which are the two aspects of man's personal drama.

At the beginning of *Burnt Norton*, we read that 'the leaves were full of children' and at the end of *Little Gidding* we read that 'the children in the apple tree' were 'not known, because not looked for'. The tree of Eden is at the source of the world, and the children who inhabit it are those beings possessed by that immediate kind of love which is innocency, by the deep intuition which accompanies original love and permits a breathless lucidity concerning the purpose and the actions of man. The children in the Parsifal story know the way to the grail castle because they are pure, and the children in Eliot's poems are still waiting for the modern quester to recover sufficient innocency to ask for the way. In Mr Pavel Tchelitchew's painting *Cache-Cache*, completed in 1942 and now exhibited in the Museum of Modern Art in New York, the same subject reappears invested with a dramatic anguish which illumines the entire theme of the children in the tree.

Childhood is that period when man's mission of fidelity is easy and natural to accomplish. And since the tree of knowledge is the eternalized symbol of God's fidelity to man, there exists an intimate relation between the child and the tree. The child understands the tree without needing to understand the knowledge of the tree. As the vegetable and the mineral do not dissimulate any one of the elements with which they are composed, so the child has no need of hiding its life which is one with that of the tree. Tchelitchew's genius has fused the faces of hundreds of children with the leaves and the flowers. *Cache-Cache* is a vast painting of metamorphosis and symbolism, comparable in its complexity to *Ulysses* and *Finnegans Wake*. Two opposing principles are at work everywhere on the canvas: first, the process by which nature imitates the coarseness or at least the terror of man in the resemblance between the tree (its trunk, roots, and branches) and the bones and nails of some monstrous hand; and secondly, the process by which the children, who represent the human species, are being transformed into the tree and therefore into a non-human species. The tree and the child are both being transformed simultaneously and to the same degree, and they are both undergoing a simultaneous torture and liberation.

As in the dawns of the earliest days of the world, the children in *Cache-Cache* are rushing toward one another, blindly, the same blood in their veins animating them, the same desperate love and fate joining them. Liturgical colours mark the children's encirclement of the seasons. A testicle and a fœtus indicate at the bottom of the tree the male and female origin of life, and, at the top, wheat and an apple symbolize the apex and fruition of life. The figure of the little girl in the centre of the picture, pressing her face against the trunk and counting out the seconds in the game of *Hide and Seek*, is the hero, a kind of Hamlet gone child. She and the small boy to her right appear to be fornicating with the tree rather than with themselves in their sprawled attitude which is an effort to lose themselves in nature. Tchelitchew's children in the tree, Parsifal lost in the dry places of the world, Hamlet in his father's castle, and the poet Eliot in his memory of the rose garden and in the reality of Little Gidding are all seeking to identify themselves. But self-identification and self-annihilation are regions extraordinarily close one to the other. As there is no interval between day and night, there is no intermediary hope or risk between the hope of salvation and the risk of destruction.

Thus, in the children, meet the two worlds of hope and fear, of knowledge and ignorance, of success and failure. A little girl in *Cache-Cache* is blindfolded, but no more so than Hamlet, and the children in the poem are unknown because unseen. Tchelitchew and Eliot have both composed works which are simultaneously a cycle and a drama. Their memory of pure childhood provides the cycle, and the memory of the agonized search for the world in childhood and the subsequent desperate search for the child in adulthood provide the drama. Both the poet and the painter have been guided by the children, and in each case the artist is depicted against the background of the awful lucidity of children. The inner landscapes of the children, which are their dream and their horror, are recast by the artist who, alone in the society of man, remains the child in his power of metamorphosis and symbolism.

iii   *fire: symbolism of love*
                    '*One Song, one Bridge of Fire*'—Hart Crane

There is fire in *Cache-Cache*, at the conclusion of the cycle. Fire and winter are joined into one moment and one substance in Tchelitchew's painting, as they become one in the midwinter spring of Eliot's *Little Gidding* when 'the brief sun flames the ice'. (part I.) The end of the year and the end of time are consumed by fire, but the end and the fire are also a beginning. The leaves of Tchelitchew's tree which gradually change colour until they burst into the tiny flames of the final fire resemble the roses of Eliot's poem which are, at the end, converted into tongues of flames. Fire is at the creation of human love in its energizing phallic sun symbolism, and it is likewise at the completion of human love, when, despite the coldness and age of love, it is consumed in its winter flames as in the vast maternal breast of the earth itself.

Here, in the ultimate combustion of nature, in what Gerard Manley Hopkins calls 'a Heraclitean Fire and the comfort of the Resurrection' (*Poems*, p. 67), the three orders of love are joined, the philosophical, divine and human, and in the new union the divine embraces all and explains all. Man's entire existence tends toward that moment when the fire of Christ's love ignites his own substance and in the new flames becomes an indistinguishable part of Christ's love. It is the moment described by Hopkins in the line 'I am all at once what Christ is', and described by Eliot in the third part of *Little Gidding* as the transfiguration of self 'in another pattern'.

The order we establish here of philosophical, divine, and human love has its own reason. Divine love is generated at the coming together, from two opposite directions, of the knowledge of love, which is philosophical, and the experience of love, which is human. Centrally fixed and burning, Divine Love needs on one side the abstract knowledge and desire of Itself, and on its other side the flame of human love and suffering: It must draw on desire and experience for its own transcended desire and transcendental experience.

In Mallarmé's *Pitre Châtié* the sun strikes the lover in a flame of warning and chastening admonishment. In Valéry's *Cimetière Marin* the immobility of the sun is compared to that of the dead absorbed into the permanency of matter, the fixed element in the revolving cycle of time and life. In Plotinus' first *Ennead*, fire is the one element that exists alone and refuses to allow the cohabitation of any other element: 'It is alone and does not welcome the other elements'. (i.vi.3.) In the final line of *Little Gidding* when the rose and the fire are one, that is, when the love of man and the love of God are merged, knowledge and love are united in the unique element of fire, and the end of man, which is his divinization in Christ, is achieved.

Love, in its purely human manifestation, as seen in Héloise, in Phèdre, and in Cleopatra, is a defiance of the world and the principle of the world. Christian love also defies the world, but at the same time it affirms Christ. To love is to forego everything that is normal, casual, and comfortable. The child, in his pallid innocency, knows the premonition of love as he wanders through the utter loneliness of his rose garden. The clown, under his white greasepaint, mimics the strategy of love, as he races through the flaming hoop, alone, but watched by his thousand-eyed public. The child and the clown, in their real and fictional whiteness, exist alone in their fervour, but at certain moments of deep social consciousness groups and nations and even entire civilizations are fused into a unified spirit in their contemplation of the child and the clown.

The paradox of love is completely expressed in the paradox of the Nativity. The Child came into the loneliness and emptiness of the world, and yet shepherds of the earth as well as angelic hosts rejoiced at the beginning of the saddest and most tragic life. The Incarnation of God's Love was preceded by its age-long desire in the hearts of the chosen people and followed by all the lesser experiences of love which crowd the days and stifle the nights of mankind. As fire from the star over Bethlehem marked the Manger, so fire from the sun of the resurrection fell upon the Cross and outlined the clear silhouette of the Clown hanging there. Before the manger Infant and the crucified Lord, the same crowd continues to pray yearly, in trying to adore and pierce the contained love of the Child and the Clown.

INDEX

Abélard 8, 29-36, 49
Apollinaire 65, 76, 80-96
Aquinas, S. Thomas 11, 12, 17, 27, 101
Aragon 65
Aristotle 16, 37, 112
Athanatius 17
Augustine, St. 8, 16, 17, 31, 38, 45, 46,
   70, 71, 85, 98, 104, 116

Barnes 139-146
Baudelaire 46, 47, 67, 73, 79, 85, 87,
   92, 136, 138, 145
Belitt 115
Bergson 108
Bernard, St. 8, 9, 22-29, 30, 35, 45, 46,
   49, 50, 78, 85
Blake 66, 79
Bloy 65
Boethius 45
Bossuet 30
Braque 65, 93
Breton 65
Brinnin 115
Byron 122

Calvin 76
Cavalcanti 25
Cézanne 11, 94, 95, 96, 107, 115
Chagall 70, 95
Chaplin 11, 95, 132
Chateaubriand 30, 58
Chirico 70, 90
Claudel 49, 50, 112, 128, 130
Cocteau 12, 76, 77, 95, 115, 126
Corneille 37-44, 51, 57, 63
Crane, Hart 12, 56, 87, 94, 115, 128-
   138
Crashaw 124

Dante 11, 22, 23-26, 33, 34, 46, 47, 66,
   67, 77, 87, 98, 100, 101, 104, 105,
   131, 144, 148
Debussy 145
Descartes 34, 42, 44
Dickinson 145, 146
Dostoievsky 67
Ducasse 65

Einstein 108
Eliot 11, 13, 46, 65, 91, 95, 130, 131,
   146-154
Eluard 65
Euripides 37

Flaubert 83, 116
Fokine 115
François de Sales, S. 85
Freud 38, 42, 121
Frijsh 145, 146

Gide 49, 50, 145
Graham 145, 146
Gregory, S. 17
Guinizelli 25

Héloise 29-36
Holderlin 67
Hopkins 128, 130, 136 153
Hugo 49, 64, 67, 79, 87

Jacob, Max 65
James, Wm. 131
John of the Cross, St. 66, 111
Joyce 11, 13, 14, 46, 48, 60, 65, 67,
   88, 96-109, 117, 145

Kierkegaard 38, 39, 46
Kolbe 12

Laforgue 11, 91
Lamartine 58
Landowska 146
Laurencin 90, 92, 93
Lautréamont 64-73, 76

Mallarmé 10-14, 65, 68, 95, 110, 115,
   123, 149, 153
Mann 116
Matisse 93
Matta 70
Mauriac 46, 84
Melville 129
Michelangelo 135
Miller 145
Milton 98, 131

Mistinguett 95
Montaigne 45, 49, 50
Musset 58

Navarre, Marguerite de 46
Nazimova 146
Nerval 58-63, 64, 67, 73, 79, 91, 111
Nietzsche 76

Ovid 25

Pascal 44-51, 57, 66, 79, 90, 98
Péguy 136
Perse, St.-John 87
Picasso 11, 48, 65, 68, 89, 90, 93, 94,
    107, 115
Pirandello 106
Plato 9, 15, 16, 37, 45-47, 114
Plotinus 8, 15-22, 23, 24, 26, 27, 35,
    45, 63, 79, 107, 154
Porphory 16, 20, 45
Proust 12, 62, 96-109, 110, 124, 128

Rabelais 45, 46, 105
Racine 51-57, 77, 98, 108, 139
Renan 30, 67
Rilke 130, 146
Rimbaud 48, 49, 64, 65, 71-73, 76,
    88-96, 111, 125, 128-138, 147
Rouault 11, 94, 115
Rousseau 63, 67, 76

Sade 66
Saint-Exupéry 109-113
Sand 64, 103, 104
Santayana 46
Satie 94
Scève 128
Shakespeare 55, 105, 107, 108, 135
Socrates 16
Sophocles 11, 37, 108
Soupault 91
Stendhal 64, 109, 121
Stravinsky 94, 115

Tchelitchew 47, 48, 148-154

Valéry 153
Verlaine 47, 86, 87, 91, 150
Vico 101 104
Villon 80-96
Voltaire 45, 67

Watteau 94
Welty 117
Whitehead 108
Whitman 79, 132, 142

Yeats 131

Zola 67

MIDLAND BOOKS

MB-1	OVID'S METAMORPHOSES *translated by Rolfe Humphries*	
	(cloth $4.95)	$1.95
MB-2	OVID'S THE ART OF LOVE *translated by Rolfe Humphries*	$1.85
MB-3	THE LOVE ETHIC OF D. H. LAWRENCE *by Mark Spilka*	$1.75
MB-4	SANTAYANA AND THE SENSE OF BEAUTY *by Willard Arnett*	$1.85
MB-5	THE EXAMINED LIFE *by Warner Fite*	$1.95
MB-6	THE DIPLOMACY OF THE AMERICAN REVOLUTION *by Samuel Flagg Bemis*	$1.95
MB-7	THE LITERARY SYMBOL *by William York Tindall*	$1.75
MB-8	GEOFFREY CHAUCER *by John Livingston Lowes*	$1.95
MB-9	THE EMPEROR'S CLOTHES *by Kathleen Nott*	$1.75
MB-10	IN THE SPIRIT OF WILLIAM JAMES *by Ralph Barton Perry*	$1.50
MB-11	SKETCH FOR A SELF-PORTRAIT *by Bernard Berenson*	$1.50
MB-12	THE DOUBLE *by F. M. Dostoyevsky*	$1.75
MB-13	PAUL GAUGUIN'S INTIMATE JOURNALS *translated and edited by Van Wyck Brooks* (52 illustrations) (cloth $3.95)	$1.95
MB-14	AFRICAN NOTEBOOK *by Albert Schweitzer* (cloth $3.95)	$1.60
MB-15	THE MORAL DECISION *by Edmond Cahn* (cloth $5.00)	$2.25
MB-16	FORMS OF MODERN FICTION *edited by William Van O'Connor*	$1.75
MB-17	FIVE MASTERS: A STUDY IN THE MUTATIONS OF THE NOVEL *by Joseph Wood Krutch*	$1.75
MB-19	THE ESTHETIC BASIS OF GREEK ART *by Rhys Carpenter* (illustrated)	$1.75
MB-20	THE SATIRES OF JUVENAL *translated by Rolfe Humphries* (cloth $3.75)	$1.65
MB-21	FREEDOM AND CIVILIZATION *by Bronislaw Malinowski*	$2.25
MB-22	JOHN DRYDEN: A STUDY OF HIS POETRY *by Mark Van Doren*	$1.75
MB-23	THE MANAGERIAL REVOLUTION *by James Burnham*	$1.95
MB-24	AGE OF SURREALISM *by Wallace Fowlie* (illustrated)	$1.75
MB-25	COLERIDGE ON IMAGINATION *by I. A. Richards*	$1.75
MB-26	JAMES JOYCE AND THE MAKING OF ULYSSES *by Frank Budgen*	$1.95
MB-27	THE LIFE OF SCIENCE *by George Sarton, introduction by Conway Zirkle*	$1.50
MB-28	OUR AMERICAN WEATHER *by George H. T. Kimble* (illustrated)	$1.95
MB-29	THE THREE WORLDS OF ALBERT SCHWEITZER *by Robert Payne*	$1.75
MB-30	OXFORD LECTURES ON POETRY *by A. C. Bradley*	$2.45
MB-31	ASPECTS OF FORM *edited by Lancelot Law Whyte*	$1.95
MB-32	ART AND INDUSTRY *by Herbert Read* (138 illustrations)	$1.95
MB-33	THE TALES OF RABBI NACHMAN *by Martin Buber, translated by Maurice Friedman*	$1.95
MB-34	MAGIC AND SCHIZOPHRENIA *by Géza Róheim* (cloth $5.00)	$2.25
MB-35	THE HISTORY OF SCIENCE AND THE NEW HUMANISM *by George Sarton*	$1.95
MB-36	THE GOLDEN ASS *by Apuleius, translated by Jack Lindsay*	$1.85
MB-37	MUSIC IN AMERICAN LIFE *by Jacques Barzun*	$1.75
MB-38	DANTE'S LA VITA NUOVA *translated by Mark Musa*	$1.65
MB-39	NEHRU ON WORLD HISTORY *condensed by Saul K. Padover from* Glimpses of World History *by Jawaharlal Nehru*	$2.45
MB-40	THE DISCOVERY OF LANGUAGE: LINGUISTIC SCIENCE IN THE NINETEENTH CENTURY *by Holger Pedersen, tr. by John Webster Spargo* (illustrated) (cloth $6.50)	$2.95

(continued on next page)

MB-41 THE PARADOX OF TRAGEDY *by D. D. Raphael* (cloth $3.00) $1.45

MB-42 AN INTRODUCTION TO THE GREEK THEATRE *by Peter D. Arnott* $2.45

MB-43 REFLECTIONS ON THE DEATH OF A PORCUPINE *by D. H. Lawrence* $1.95

MB-44 THE THREE WORLDS OF BORIS PASTERNAK *by Robert Payne* $1.95

MB-45 VERGIL'S AENEID *translated, with an introduction and notes by L. R. Lind* (cloth $5.75) $1.95

MB-46 ESSAYS ON THE ODYSSEY: SELECTED MODERN CRITICISM *edited by Charles H. Taylor, Jr.* (cloth $6.00) $1.95

MB-47 THE LIVING THOUGHTS OF KIERKEGAARD *presented by W. H. Auden* $1.95

MB-48 THE QUESTION OF JEAN-JACQUES ROUSSEAU *by Ernst Cassirer, translated and edited by Peter Gay* $1.65

MB-49 THE NEW APOLOGISTS FOR POETRY *by Murray Krieger* $2.25

MB-50 SPEECH: ITS FUNCTION AND DEVELOPMENT *by Grace Andrus de Laguna* (cloth $6.50) $2.95

MB-51 ARIOSTO'S ORLANDO FURIOSO: SELECTIONS FROM SIR JOHN HARINGTON'S TRANSLATION *edited by Rudolf Gottfried* (cloth $6.50) $2.95

MB-52 THE ENCHIRIDION OF ERASMUS *translated with an introduction by Raymond Himelick* (cloth $6.00) $2.45

MB-53 MARTIAL: SELECTED EPIGRAMS *translated by Rolfe Humphries, introduction by Palmer Bovie* (illustrated) (cloth $5.00) $1.95

MB-54 THE IDIOM OF POETRY *by Frederick A. Pottle* $1.95

MB-55 THE SENSE OF INJUSTICE *by Edmond Cahn* $1.75

MB-56 MANKIND, NATION AND INDIVIDUAL FROM A LINGUISTIC POINT OF VIEW *by Otto Jespersen* (cloth $4.50) $1.95

MB-57 D. H. LAWRENCE: THE FAILURE AND THE TRIUMPH OF ART *by Eliseo Vivas* $2.25

MB-58 THE CHALLENGE OF EXISTENTIALISM *by John Wild* (cloth $6.00) $1.95

MB-59 THE JOURNALS OF JEAN COCTEAU *edited and translated with an introduction by Wallace Fowlie* (illustrated) $1.95

MB-60 THREE GREEK PLAYS FOR THE THEATRE *translated by Peter D. Arnott* (cloth $5.00) $1.95

MB-61 THE AMERICAN NEGRO *by Melville J. Herskovits* $1.65

MB-62 THE CHINESE EYE: AN INTERPRETATION OF CHINESE PAINTING *by Chiang Yee* (illustrated) $2.45

MB-63 PERSPECTIVES BY INCONGRUITY *by Kenneth Burke, edited by Stanley Edgar Hyman* (MB-63 and 64 comb. cloth $6.95) $2.45

MB-64 TERMS FOR ORDER *by Kenneth Burke, edited by Stanley Edgar Hyman* (MB-63 and 64 comb. cloth $6.95) $2.45

MB-65 EARLY MEDIEVAL ART *by Ernst Kitzinger* (48 plates) $1.95

MB-66 THE RAMPAGING FRONTIER *by Thomas D. Clark* (cloth $6.00) $2.45

MB-67 A STYLE MANUAL FOR STUDENTS: BASED ON THE MLA STYLE SHEET *by Edward D. Seeber* $1.00

MB-68 ESSAYS IN THE PHILOSOPHY OF ART *by R. G. Collingwood, edited with an introduction by Alan Donagan* (cloth $6.00) $2.45

MB-69 ESSAYS ON DANTE *edited by Mark Musa* (cloth $6.00) $2.45

MB-70 THE INFLUENCE OF DARWIN ON PHILOSOPHY *by John Dewey* $2.45

MB-71 RATIONAL MAN: A MODERN INTERPRETATION OF ARISTOTELIAN ETHICS *by Henry B. Veatch* (cloth $5.00) $1.95

MB-72 THE STATURE OF THEODORE DREISER: A CRITICAL SURVEY OF THE MAN AND HIS WORK *edited by Alfred Kazin and Charles Shapiro* $2.25

MB-73 BEOWULF *translated by Lucien Dean Pearson, edited with an introduction and notes by Rowland L. Collins* (cloth $6.00) $1.95

MB-74 LOVE IN LITERATURE: STUDIES IN SYMBOLIC EXPRESSION *by Wallace Fowlie* $1.65

MB-75 THE POPULATION CRISIS: IMPLICATIONS AND PLANS FOR ACTION *edited by Larry K. Y. Ng, with Stuart Mudd, Co-Editor* $2.95

MB-76 A STYLE MANUAL FOR AUTHORS *by Edward D. Seeber* $1.25